Who Wants to Run?

Chicago Studies in American Politics

A SERIES EDITED BY BENJAMIN I. PAGE, SUSAN HERBST,
LAWRENCE R. JACOBS, AND ADAM J. BERINSKY

Also in the series:

Additional series titles follow index

Who Wants to Run?

*How the Devaluing of Political Office
Drives Polarization*

ANDREW B. HALL

THE UNIVERSITY OF CHICAGO PRESS   CHICAGO AND LONDON

The University of Chicago Press, Chicago 60637
The University of Chicago Press, Ltd., London
Published 2019
Printed in the United States of America

28 27 26 25 24 23 22 21 20 19   1 2 3 4 5

ISBN-13: 978-0-226-60943-0 (cloth)
ISBN-13: 978-0-226-60957-7 (paper)
ISBN-13: 978-0-226-60960-7 (e-book)
DOI: https://doi.org/10.7208/chicago/9780226609607.001.0001

Library of Congress Cataloging-in-Publication Data

Names: Hall, Andrew B., author.
Title: Who wants to run? : how the devaluing of political office drives
    polarization / Andrew B. Hall.
Other titles: Chicago studies in American politics.
Description: Chicago ; London : The University of Chicago Press, 2019. |
Series: Chicago studies in American politics
Identifiers: LCCN 2018029190 | ISBN 9780226609430 (cloth : alk. paper) |
    ISBN 9780226609577 (pbk. : alk. paper) | ISBN 9780226609607 (e-book)
Subjects: LCSH: Political candidates—United States. |
    Elections—United States. | Polarization (Social sciences) |
    Right and left (Political science)—United States.
Classification: LCC JK1976 .H355 2019 | DDC 324.973—dc23
LC record available at https://lccn.loc.gov/2018029190

♾ This paper meets the requirements of ANSI/NISO Z39.48–1992 (Permanence of Paper).

FOR CHARLIE

Contents

Acknowledgments

I have accrued many debts since 2010 as I have worked on this project. I have been fortunate to have had the chance to work with Adam Berinsky and Chuck Myers. I have very much appreciated their wisdom, honesty, and patience. Two anonymous reviewers read the book extremely carefully and gave me detailed comments. The final version of the book is an almost complete rewrite from the initial version, and is I think much better, thanks to the efforts of the reviewers. Steve Haber and Paul Sniderman gave me invaluable guidance throughout the book process, and I am indebted to them for their wise counsel.

I owe a huge debt to Gary King, Ken Shepsle, and Jim Snyder at Harvard. The influence of all three shows through clearly in the pages of this book. In addition, I gratefully acknowledge Jeff Frieden, who originally pushed me to develop a theory of who runs for office. Too many others to name had an impact on my time at Harvard—I thank them all. And I thank the Government Department for taking a chance on me when so many other programs (perhaps reasonably) chose not to admit a classics major with a 3.2 GPA to a political science PhD program many years ago.

In the summer of 2016, Stanford Political Science kindly funded a book conference for me. Adam Berinsky, Chris Berry, Brandice Canes-Wrone, Nolan McCarty, and Marc Meredith were extremely generous with their time, and their feedback has formed the core of the revisions I have made throughout this process. I am also grateful to the many members of my own department who participated in the conference or otherwise gave me feedback, including Adam Bonica, Lisa Blaydes, Dave Brady, Bruce Cain, Gary Cox, Lauren Davenport, Jim Fearon, Vicky Fouka, Judy Goldstein, Saad Gulzar, Jens Hainmueller, Shanto Iyengar, David Laitin, Clayton Nall, Josh Ober, Jonathan Rodden, Ken Scheve, Mike Tomz, Barry Weingast, and

Jeremy Weinstein. I particularly want to thank Jackie Sargent for all of her advice and support as I have made the transition to being a faculty member at Stanford. Life in the department would be inconceivable without her.

At various points in the process, I also received extremely helpful comments from Pam Ban, Andy Eggers, Ryan Enos, Dan Hopkins, Keith Krehbiel, Chloe Lim, John Marshall, Dan Moskowitz, Max Palmer, Julia Payson, Molly Roberts, Brandon Stewart, Danielle Thomsen, and Jesse Yoder. And I enthusiastically thank Yanchen Song for excellent research assistance.

This book, not to mention my life, has been deeply shaped by my collaborators. This project largely reflects things that I have learned from these collaborators (which I hope, depending on how people view this book, will be seen as the compliment it's intended to be.)

James Feigenbaum, Michael Gill, and Connor Huff have been constant friends from the beginning of this project. Dan Thompson took notes for me at the conference and since then has collaborated with me on a number of projects, some of which have entered this book in various ways. His comments have reshaped chapter 2, in particular, and have made it much better. Alex Fouirnaies, my coauthor on many projects, helped me rewrite the introduction to this book, gave me advice on a variety of the analyses throughout the book, and, as always, has supported me with genial goodwill and camaraderie at every turn. No one could possibly ask for a better collaborator or friend.

I owe a particularly large debt to Avi Acharya, whose ideas and suggestions populate much of chapter 1. It is a joy and a privilege to have such an intellectually curious and generous—and ridiculously well read—colleague. Likewise, the impact of Adam Bonica's work, as well as his comments and suggestions, is impossible to miss in this book. My work is only possible because of his, and I and field are fortunate that he is such a helpful and generous creator of knowledge.

Justin Grimmer has shaped this book in profound ways. He has read almost every chapter, and I have overhauled each based on his invaluable comments. He has taught me to communicate more clearly and, as a result, to think more clearly. If the book is able to convince the reader of its points, it is only because of Justin. He is a model of what an academic and an intellectual colleague, and a friend, is supposed to be. I cannot thank him enough for his help and support.

Anthony Fowler has taught me much of what I know about studying politics with data. It's impossible for me to imagine my life or my work without his influence and friendship. Each analysis in this book owes something to him—some because he suggested them, directly, others because I arrived at them based on ideas and concepts that he first taught me. I don't think it is possible for anyone to meet the scientific standards or clarity of thought that Anthony achieves in his own work, but I have done my best to emulate them.

This book wouldn't be possible without the data that Jim Snyder makes so widely available to the discipline—to say nothing of how deeply he has influenced me as an advisor, frequent collaborator, and friend. His impact on me, and many of my colleagues, is without measure.

My parents and stepparents may not be political scientists, but it is only because of them that I have been able to become one. My life has been full of books since I was born. I never thought I would write a book myself, but I know that I never would have without my parents' love and support—and their innate love of reading, which they have imparted to me.

My first (and as of now, only) child, Charlie, is nine months old as I write this. When I hold books in his lap, his instinct is still to eat them rather than to read them. When he learns to read, I know that this book will not be first on his reading list. But in time, when he's curious about what his dad does for a living, I hope that he'll flip to this page and know that, whatever I do, I do it now for him.

And finally, to my wife, Alisa, it is hard to articulate the gratitude and love I feel for you every day. This book is as much yours as mine. Maybe it offers a few little ideas for how to improve our political system, but if the world were full of Alisas, it would need no improving.

Those Fittest for the Trust

And of what kind are the men [or women] that will strive for this profitable preeminence, through all the bustle of cabal, the heat of contention, the infinite mutual abuse of parties, tearing to pieces the best of characters? It will not be the wise and moderate, the lovers of peace and good order, the men [or women] fittest for the trust.—Benjamin Franklin, *Dangers of a Salaried Bureaucracy*

You'd have to be crazy to run for Congress.—Steven Latourette (R-OH), interviewed on *The Daily Show*

On November 16, 2013, newly elected Democratic members of the United States Congress, joining the U.S. House of Representatives at a time of unprecedented ideological polarization, sat down to view a presentation by the Democratic Congressional Campaign Committee (DCCC) on how they should allocate their time as first-term incumbents. On a slide entitled "Model Daily Schedule," the presenter suggested that new members should plan to dedicate four hours per day to "Call Time," time set aside for making fundraising calls, and another one hour per day to "Strategic Outreach," other forms of in-person fundraising. This is a tremendous amount of time to devote to an activity that is almost uniformly regarded as abhorrent. Reacting to the slides, Rep. John Larson (D-CT) told the *Huffington Post*, "You might as well be putting bamboo shoots under my fingernails" (Grim and Siddiqui 2017).[1] Describing the off-site call centers that members of Congress use for these activities, Rep. Peter DeFazio (D-OR) told *This American Life*, "If you walked in there, you would say, boy, this is about the worst looking, most abusive call center situation I've seen in my life" (Glass 2012). Rep. Donna Edwards (D-MD) summed up the current state of legislative politics in an interview with *Esquire*: "It's a never-ending hustle. You get elected to this august body to fix problems, and for the privilege, you find yourself on the phone in a cubicle, dialing for dollars" (Warren 2014).

The profound costs of running for Congress and the diminished appeal of being in Congress have not gone unnoticed. Indeed, would-be candidates are keenly aware of the situation. As an anonymous member of Congress told Vox.com, *"The best people don't run for Congress. Smart people figured this out years ago and decided to pursue careers other than running for Congress. The thought of living in a fishbowl with 30-second attack ads has made Congress repulsive to spouses and families. The idea of spending half your life begging rich people you don't know for money turns off all reasonable, self-respecting people. That, plus lower pay than a first-year graduate of a top law school, means that Congress . . . is not attracting the best and the brightest in America"* (A Member of Congress 2015, emphasis mine). Almost daily, we hear further news about the historic unpopularity of Congress as it achieves new heights of polarization. At least four major news outlets have run articles in recent years with the headline "Why Would Anyone Run for Congress?" or an extremely similar variant.[2]

If we want to understand why our legislatures have become so polarized, dysfunctional, and unpopular, we must answer this question.

"Who Wants to Run?" and Polarization

The point of this book is that the question "who wants to run?" is vital for understanding polarization in our legislatures, yet it is largely absent from the academic literatures on elections, ideology, and polarization. But my purpose isn't only to ask this question; it's also to offer a different way of thinking about elections and ideology that allows us to start answering it. This way of thinking promotes the use of large-scale quantitative data sets on candidate ideology and electoral outcomes, combined with modern statistical techniques for measurement and for determining causation, to understand who wants to run for office.

Most political science studies of elections and polarization focus on the behavior of voters. Important work in this vein, which I review in chapter 1, points to a variety of potential sources of legislative polarization, including changing voter preferences, redistricting, primary elections, campaign finance, and the media. All are thought to influence whom voters pick for office and to encourage the success of more extreme candidates.

But, as I will show in chapter 1, the majority of the polarization we observe in the U.S. House—defined as the ideological distance between the two parties—is *not* the result of voters choosing extreme candidates for office. Using a simulation based on work by Bonica (2017), I show that even if voters chose the most moderate candidate in every election for the U.S. House since 1980, polarization would still be extremely high. *Most legislative polarization is already baked into the set of people who run for office.* Indeed, when we look at the ideological positions of who runs for the House, we see that the set of all candidates—not just incumbents—has polarized markedly since 1980.

These facts are the jumping-off point for the way I propose to think about elections and ideology. I think of candidates as possessing ideological *types*, rather than as unconstrained actors who fluidly adapt their ideological positions as they go. A large body of research in American politics, which I will review in chapter 1, supports the idea that candidates are relatively rigid in their ideological positions. Thinking of candidates this way casts new emphasis on who runs for office, because in such a world, ideological change in our legislatures happens mainly when ideologically distinct candidates run for office and find support among voters.

A Theory for Why the Candidate Pool Polarizes

After establishing that "who wants to run?" is a key question to ask to understand polarization in the U.S. House, the latter part of chapter 1 offers a theory—simply an adaptation of so-called citizen-candidate models (Besley and Coate 1997; Osborne and Slivinski 1996)—to explain why the choice to seek office varies across the ideological spectrum. I motivate this theory with a thought experiment which is easy to follow and requires no math.

The theory supposes that citizens whose ideological positions range from the far left to the far right face certain costs of running for office, as well as certain benefits of holding office if they win election. But, because the winning candidate gets to influence ideological policies in the legislature, the ideological payoffs of running for office are not equal across the ideological spectrum. More-extreme citizens are more averse to having a representative from the opposite side of the ideological spectrum, while more-moderate citizens are more ambivalent. As a result, when costs of running are high or benefits of holding office are low, more-moderate candidates are disproportionately less likely to run.

The theory intentionally focuses on the most fundamental component of ideological polarization: the ideological positions held by individual citizens who consider seeking political office. It purposefully omits many of the more complicated factors that receive so much scrutiny in the American politics literature, such as partisanship in the electorate (e.g., Achen and Bartels 2016a) and the activities of elite actors in the district and in national politics (e.g., Cohen, Noel, and Zaller 2008; Noel 2014; Rosenfeld 2017). In many cases, considering these factors only strengthens my arguments. But what is more important is that such a simple theory appears to capture an important dynamic about who runs for political office in reality, as the empirical results throughout the book will show. The simplicity of the theory is what allows us to think clearly about how who runs for office drives polarization, and about why the set of people who run for the House is so polarized in recent times.

A New Framework for Studying Elections and Ideology

Whether more-moderate candidates possess an electoral advantage in the United States is a matter of passionate debate. Despite how important this debate is for understanding polarization, the discipline has made little progress toward resolving it. Doing so is a necessity for this book. If the fact that moderate citizens are not running for office is to help explain legislative polarization, it must be the case that they would win office if they ran.

Accordingly, the next part of the book works to explain why political science has failed to come to agreement about the links between candidate ideology and electoral success. To resolve this disagreement, I offer a new, comprehensive analysis—based on studying the electoral performance of 24,123 candidates for the House whose ideological positions are estimated using records from more than six million donors—that shows that moderate candidates are indeed advantaged in U.S. House races.

I start by considering how to study candidate ideology and elections when the goal is to shed light on what drives legislative polarization. Much of the existing research on candidate positions and electoral results attempts to estimate how much more or less vote share a candidate would receive if he or she made his or her ideological positions more moderate (or more extreme)—what the literature might call a causal effect of candidate positioning. As chapter 2 will make clear, to see whether our legislatures are polarizing because of the choices voters make in elections, we do not actually want to isolate the effect of candidate ideology itself. If all extreme candidates are tall, and voters based their choices on greater candidate height, then the legislature would polarize even though the voters were not voting because of ideology.

Instead, we want to focus on what I call *electoral selection*: the question of whether electorates choose more-moderate or less-moderate candidates for office, regardless of whether these choices are made because of candidates' ideological positions.

Actually estimating electoral selection effects is difficult in practice because it requires measures of the ideological positions of all candidates, not just winning candidates. Most existing techniques rely on roll-call votes to scale incumbents, but we cannot use these techniques to measure the ideology of people who have never won office. To solve this problem, I employ a variety of methods that use the mix of campaign contributions that candidates receive to estimate their ideology, whether or not they have served in office before. I devote significant time to discussing these scalings, justifying their validity, and explaining how we can use them to estimate the process of electoral selection. To ensure that my results do not depend on the particular flaws in any particular scaling technique, I show that all of my main conclusions are consistent across scaling methods. As such, while no analysis can ever be perfect, the findings are not the result of any particular flaw in any particular technique for using campaign contributions to estimate candidate ideology, such as the possibility of strategic donating or the risk that the scalings detect partisanship instead of ideology.

Having laid out my empirical framework for studying candidate ideology and electoral success, I implement it in chapter 3. The conclusion of these analyses is that moderate candidates possess a clear advantage in U.S. House elections. Legislative polarization in the House is not the result of general-election voters favoring more-extreme candidates—actually, electorates prefer to elect more-moderate candidates, on average. This is why studying who runs is so important for understanding polarization.

Evidence That Costs and Benefits Affect Who Runs

The first half of the book is about how we think about elections and ideology. It is where I build up the idea that "who wants to run?" is a useful way to think about ideological polarization in the U.S. House, and where I show evidence that the premises of my argument are met. The second half of the book is about marshaling evidence that the theory makes valid predictions about the political process. It is here that I will try to convince the reader not just that the theory fits some simple facts about American politics but also that it offers us new insight into how we can reduce polarization by altering the costs and benefits of running for office.

I start in chapter 4 by offering evidence for the claim that we have devalued the House over time—that is, that the costs of running for the House have increased, over time, and that the benefits of holding office have declined. I focus first on the growing burdens of campaign finance, which, as the anecdote at the beginning of this chapter suggested, seems to prevent many moderate people from running for office. I also discuss how privacy concerns due to media coverage may deter moderate candidates. Finally, I talk about how the benefits of office, both in terms of monetary compensation and in terms of opportunities to influence policy, have fallen in recent decades.

Testing the main predictions of the theory empirically is difficult because the full costs and benefits of office can never be observed. The tests in chapters 5 and 6 try to circumvent this issue by exploiting situations in which a particular, observable component of the costs or benefits varies in a way that is plausibly independent from all the other unobserved components of the costs and benefits.

I start by studying salary reforms in state legislatures, using new data on salaries collected from primary sources. When state legislatures pay their legislators more, more-moderate people appear to run for office at higher rates, and legislatures seem to become less polarized as a result. Next, I look at who runs for the House when an incumbent holds a seat— which makes it harder to run and to win office—compared with open seats. More-moderate people run when they can do so without challenging an incumbent, indicating again that costs and benefits affect the ideological composition of the candidate pool. Finally, I study the decision of state legislators to run for the House. When state legislators can run without giving up their current seat, more-moderate candidates become more likely to run. When they must give up their seat, a considerable cost, more-extreme candidates still run but more-moderate candidates do not.

All of these analyses are only partial, but they all point to the potentially important role that costs and benefits play in discouraging moderate candidates from running, and they are all consistent with the theoretical model I propose in chapter 1. Taken together, they demonstrate the value of focusing on "who wants to run?" to understand legislative polarization, not just in the House but in a wide variety of legislative contexts.

Policy Implications of "Who Wants to Run?"

Americans across the ideological spectrum are dissatisfied with Congress, but I do not want to overinterpret the problems of modern ideological polarization. Every era faces unique political challenges, and political scientists and pundits often overemphasize the particular issues of the day. Nevertheless, as I will discuss, ideological polarization appears to be contrary to voters' wishes, and it appears to impede the legislative process. This is part of the reason why many people seek reforms that would reduce polarization in our legislatures.

This book suggests that we have been missing some of the most promising avenues to reduce polarization. Reformers of the day are largely focused on electoral changes, especially reforms to gerrymandering, primary elections, and interest-group influence. All of these factors may be important, but all are focused on the behavior of voters rather than on who runs for office. By showing that who runs for office drives polarization in our legislatures, this book suggests that reformers interested in reducing polarization should instead think about how to make the costs of running for office lower, and about how to make the benefits of holding office higher. The purpose of this book is not to make concrete policy reforms but rather to encourage reformers to pay more attention to these costs and benefits. Candidate recruitment is central to American politics and to legislative polarization, and we would do well to spend more time thinking about how to change our politics to make candidate recruitment easier. Doing so might include paying legislators more—perhaps by creating an independent commission so that our politicians are not forced to set their own salaries—as well as changing our system of campaign finance so that candidates spend less time fundraising.

The Broader Importance of "Who Wants to Run?"

I conclude the book by discussing the broader meaning of the question "who wants to run?" for the study of American politics, and for the study of democratic politics more generally.

The free entry of citizens into political candidacy is a defining feature of American democracy, but we have not fully appreciated what it implies for our political process. Our parties are, in the end, defined by who chooses to run, and by whom voters choose to be their standard-bearers. The Tea Party revolution, for example, did not move the Republican Party to the right by persuading some imagined centralized party leadership to move right; it moved the Republican Party to the right because Tea Party candidates ran for office. These Tea Partiers were not recruited by the party—the Republican Party did not "run" them, the way many parties in parliamentary systems are often able to choose candidates to put on the ballot. They ran themselves.

Yes, American parties can draft national platforms, which almost nobody reads; they can try to recruit people to run for office, with little to offer by way of inducement; and they can attempt to influence who wins elections, using a variety of tactics we know are relatively ineffective. But at the end of the day, they are at the mercy of individual Americans' choices— the citizen's choice to become a candidate and the voter's choice to support a particular candidate in a primary or in a general election.

A person's choice to run for office is therefore central to understanding what our parties do, what choices our electorates face, and how our government functions. In this book, I will show how the incentives we have created for candidates have generated legislative polarization, but the consequences extend far beyond polarization. A young literature in political economy is just starting to grapple with the question of when and why more competent types choose to seek political office (e.g., Besley and Reynal-Querol 2011; Dal Bó et al. 2017). My book is intended to contribute an American data point to these primarily international studies and to show some of the links between studying ideological self-selection and other types of self-selection into politics.

Understanding who wants to run for office should be a fundamental question in political science. Democratic governance can function properly only when competent types who reflect the desires of their constituents stand up and seek political office. I do not intend this book to be the final answer to the question of who wants to run for office, but rather the beginning of a conversation about why who runs for office is so vitally important for understanding American politics.

CHAPTER ONE

Who Wants to Run?

If the people can choose only from among rascals, they are certain to choose a rascal.
—V. O. Key, *The Responsible Electorate*

To summarize: it is a well-known fact that those people who must want to rule people are, ipso facto, those least suited to do it.—Douglas Adams, *The Restaurant at the End of the Universe*

T he goal of this chapter is to convince you that, if you want to understand polarization in American politics, you need to ask the question: *who wants to run?*

American legislatures are in turmoil. The United States Congress is crippled by ideological disagreements and partisan rankling that make it difficult to craft new policies or to update obsolete ones. This book will not explain all the complex causes of this state of affairs, but it will explore a key factor—the willingness of individuals of varying ideologies to seek political office—that is largely absent from existing work on political polarization.

This chapter presents the overall argument in three parts. First, I document the rise of ideological polarization in the U.S. House and explain that we should care about it because it creates legislative dysfunction and appears to be contrary to voters' wishes.

Second, I discuss how existing research on legislative polarization focuses mainly on the preferences of voters rather than the behavior of candidates. I then present evidence that the preferences of voters cannot explain most of legislative polarization, or its rise. Even if voters selected the most moderate available candidates in every election since 1980, polarization in the U.S. House still would have risen roughly 80 percent as much as we have observed. To understand legislative polarization, we need to understand why the people running to become members of Congress have themselves polarized.

Third, and finally, I offer a theory, based closely on citizen-candidate models, for why some people become candidates while others do not and for how this decision contributes to polarization. The theory explains that the set of people who run for office will become more ideologically extreme when the costs of running for office are high and when the benefits of holding office are low—conditions that, I will argue in chapter 4, are increasingly met in our federal legislatures. The logic is as follows. Someone on the far left or far right will particularly dislike having a representative from the other end of the ideological spectrum and therefore will be more likely to be willing to bear the considerable costs of running for office to avoid this fate. Someone toward the middle of the ideological spectrum is not as far from extremists in either party; this person's disutility from an extremist representative is therefore not as large as it is for an extremist in one party facing an extremist representative from the other party. As a result, moderate citizens will be less willing to bear the costs of candidacy.

Rising Polarization in U.S. Legislatures

The primary focus of this book will be to explain why who runs for office has helped spur the well-documented rise in ideological polarization in our legislatures since 1980 (McCarty, Poole, and Rosenthal 2006). Figure 1.1 plots a common measure of polarization for the U.S. House (Poole and Rosenthal 2000), based on how differently members of the two parties cast roll-call votes, for the years 1879–2014. Higher values of this measure indicate greater ideological disagreement between the two parties. The pattern is obvious. Since 1980 (shaded in gray in the figure), the ideological gap between the two parties in the House has more than doubled, and it now exceeds previous all-time highs from the turn of the twentieth century.

Why is it worth explaining this recent rise? Legislative polarization is not just some statistical artifact from measuring roll-call voting behavior. Rising polarization means that the parties are systematically disagreeing more, whether due to ideological differences, partisan loyalty, or both. The result is a legislature that struggles to accomplish even the most basic tasks before it. Perhaps the clearest symptom of this issue is the budgeting process. A process once known as "Regular Order" is now "best described as 'Regular Disorder'" (McCarty 2014, 1), with Congress regularly failing to complete the budget process. Government shutdowns and brinksmanship are clear consequences of legislative polarization.

Perhaps more important, legislative polarization appears to be con-

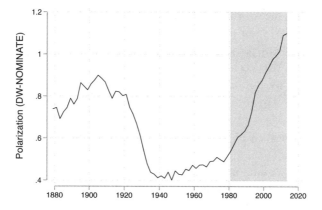

FIGURE I.I. Rising polarization in the U.S. House of Representatives. This graph plots ideological polarization in the U.S. House based on roll-call votes. Polarization has risen sharply since 1980. *Source*: Lewis et al. 2017.

trary to voters' wishes. There is considerable confusion in political science about how to study the links between elections and ideology. In chapters 2 and 3, I will explain this confusion and offer a framework for evaluating what voters prefer *based on their actual choices in real elections*. Applying this framework, I show that voters prefer more-moderate candidates in U.S. House elections, on average. I do not mean *prefer* in the sense that voters themselves necessarily espouse particular policy views that are moderate, or even that it's the candidates' positions per se that drive voters to support them—although these things may well be true. Instead, I mean it in the precise sense that, when given the choice to elect candidates who have taken more-moderate positions or to elect candidates who have taken more-extreme positions, voters tend to elect the candidates who offer more-moderate positions. If our legislatures are nevertheless populated with candidates whose positions are more extreme than those of the candidates voters seem to prefer, then our political institutions have failed to translate the desires of voters into legislative activity efficiently. Put simply, it is likely that voters would be better off—in the sense that they would change whom they elected to office—if more candidates who offer moderate platforms ran for office.

I do not mean to suggest that polarization is the only problem in current American politics, or that reducing polarization would be a panacea. And I do not mean to suggest that previous, low polarization eras in American politics reflected any sort of political utopia—indeed, the 1950s and 1960s exhibited relatively low legislative polarization but presented enormous political challenges in their own right. Nevertheless, there are gains to reducing polarization from its current, unprecedented heights. Like all political problems, polarization implies trade-offs, and reformers must always consider these trade-offs when advocating for focusing on one issue over another. I will return to this issue in the book's conclusion.

Existing Accounts of Polarization Are Votercentric

Now that I have laid out the problem to be studied, the next question is how to study it. Political scientists have largely missed how important the question "who wants to run?" is for understanding legislative polarization because we have been so focused on votercentric accounts of polarization. This is not to say that political science does not study the choice to become a candidate. Indeed, large literatures in political science study political ambition—particularly as it relates to women in politics (e.g., Kanthak and Woon 2015; Lawless and Fox 2005, 2015; Preece and Stoddard 2015; Sanbonmatsu 2010; Thomsen 2015, 2017) and to the strategic decisions of career-minded politicians (e.g., Cox and Katz 1996; L. Fowler 1993; Maestas et al. 2006; Maisel and Stone 2014)—but they do not usually consider legislative polarization directly. The exception to this rule is the work of Thomsen (2017), which makes an argument similar and complementary to this book's argument, focusing on how party fit in the legislature discourages moderates from running for the U.S. House, thereby driving polarization. I will lean heavily on this account in chapter 4. Reviewing the literature, Thomsen observes that "candidate emergence has received only minimal attention from polarization scholars" (6).

Instead, political scientists have studied the polarization of American politics in two main ways. Institutional scholars have looked to real-world behavior in the legislature, documenting the way legislators of the two parties have grown farther apart, ideologically, and evaluating links between this change and a variety of structural factors such as income inequality (McCarty, Poole, and Rosenthal 2006; Voorheis, McCarty, and Shor 2015), redistricting (Carson et al. 2007; Eilperin 2007; Masket, Winburn, and Wright 2012; McCarty, Poole, and Rosenthal 2009; Theriault 2008), and primary elections (Aranson and Ordeshook 1972; Burden 2001; Brady, Han, and Pope 2007; Coleman 1971; Hill and Tausanovitch 2017; Hirano et al. 2010; McGhee et al. 2014; Owen and Grofman 2006; Pildes 2011).

Meanwhile, behavioral scholars have looked to individual voters, measuring their political attitudes in surveys to see how they have changed over time. But even on the fundamental question of whether voters have polarized, substantial disagreement remains. To pick perhaps the most famous of these disagreements, Fiorina, Abrams, and Pope (2005) and Fiorina and Abrams (2009) argue that only a small class of political elites has polarized over time, while voters themselves have not. Abramowitz (2011) strongly disagrees, arguing that voters of the two parties have sorted in their views on a range of issues and become more extreme. To date, the disagreement rages on.

Another thread of the behavioral literature suggests that the blind partisanship of voters allows parties to pursue the ideological goals of elites without electoral sanction. In a *New York Times* op-ed, Achen and Bartels write, "That is one key reason contemporary American politics is so polarized: The electoral penalty for candidates taking extreme positions is quite modest because voters in the political center do not reliably support the candidates closest to them on the issues." This is an argument they pursue in their recent book (Achen and Bartels 2016a). In chapter 3, I document a pronounced electoral advantage for moderate candidates when we study election returns rather than surveys—but the more important point is that this account, too, is focused on voters.

Each approach, the institutional and the behavioral, has its own strengths and weaknesses, but *both* have missed how the candidate supply—the set of people willing to run for office—contributes to polarization. When institutional scholars have observed changes in legislator behavior and attributed them to external forces, they have, implicitly or explicitly, assumed that these changes relate to changes in what their constituents want. When behavioral scholars have seen changes in voter opinion and connected them to the current state of legislative politics, they have, implicitly or explicitly, assumed that these changes are reflected in the behavior of voters' representatives.[1] Both literatures study one side of the equation—either voters or legislators—and impute some kind of response to the other side. But if the set of people running for office has itself polarized, these assumptions are not necessarily met. Legislators might polarize even if voters do not want them to, because voters can only elect representatives from among the set of people who run for office.

Voter Preferences Not Enough to Explain Rising Polarization

Though there are good reasons to study voters in relation to polarization, ignoring candidates risks missing the bulk of legislative polarization. In

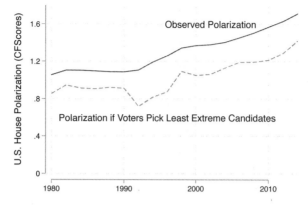

FIGURE I.2. Legislative polarization not primarily explained by voter choices. This graph compares observed legislative polarization, measured using the CFscores scaling methodology, to the level of legislative polarization we would observe if in every district the most-moderate candidates always won office. Because few moderates run for office, even if voters elected the most-moderate candidates who run, legislative polarization would still be very high.

fact, legislative polarization would still be high, and rising, even if voters always elected the most moderate possible candidate in every election cycle in every district.

Figure I.2 shows a set of simulations based closely on those developed by Bonica (2017). The first line, in solid black, plots the observed polarization in the U.S. House from 1980 through 2014, measured by scaling incumbents in terms of their ideology using the mix of campaign contributions they receive from donors (Bonica 2014). I will discuss this scaling technique, CFscores, in detail in chapter 3, where I will justify its validity as well as introduce alternate scaling methods that produce similar results. The second line, in dashed gray, plots how polarized the legislature would be if, in every election, House voters elected only the least-extreme available candidates, measured again using campaign contributions, defining *least-extreme* as the candidate scaled closest to the midpoint of the ideological scale.[2] The gray line is therefore the hypothetical least amount of polarization we could see, given the set of people who have chosen to run for the House over this period. As figure I.2 shows, even in this extreme hypothetical, we still see a very high degree of polarization. That is, even if voters always elected the most-moderate candidates they could, legislative polarization would still be very high in the U.S. House.

According to the simulation, roughly 20 percent of overall polarization in the House is due to choices voters make among the candidates who run for office. The other 80 percent of polarization exists no matter which candidates voters choose from among the existing pool—it is already baked into the set of people who run for office! *Although the literature on polarization has focused on the choices voters make among candidates, the bulk of legislative polarization may not be due to these choices.*

Voters may also contribute to polarization indirectly in ways the simulation does not capture. Some of the observed polarization could be due, for example, to moderates not running because they anticipate that voters will not support them if they do run. I will consider this possibility—and more generally, the degree to which voters support moderate candidates—in chapter 3, where I show that voters tend to elect moderates when moderates run for office. In any case, the takeaway here is not that voters' preferences do not matter but rather that who runs for office also matters a great deal for polarization.

How do we know that these simulations correctly measure candidate ideology, when they rely on campaign contributions to scale candidates? For example, what if donors are strategic, or what if the scalings are picking up partisanship rather than ideology? I will address these methodological issues in chapter 2, but I will note here that the simulation's conclusions are unchanged if we use alternative methods to measure candidate ideology. In appendix 1, I replicate this plot using DW-DIME, which uses the contributions in a machine-learning setup to predict roll-call ideology (Bonica forthcoming), an approach that addresses the issue of partisanship.[3] Using DW-DIME, the simulation estimates that 86 percent of polarization is explained by the candidate pool rather than by which candidates voters choose from among the pool. I also replicate the plot using Hall-Snyder scores, an alternative technique that omits all contributions made to candidates after they become incumbents to ensure that the scalings are not driven by strategic donating. Again, we arrive at the same conclusion. See appendix 1 for this analysis.

Candidates Becoming More Polarized

If most of polarization is due to who runs, rather than due to whom voters choose for office, then the set of people who choose to run for the House must be polarizing over time. Figure 1.3 confirms this pattern. The graph shows the absolute distance between the average ideological position of each party for each year, separately for incumbents and nonincumbents

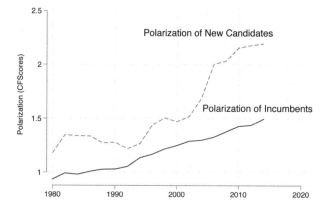

FIGURE 1.3. The growing polarization of candidates for the U.S House of Representatives, 1980–2014. Each line is the absolute difference in average CFscores across the two parties for the relevant candidate group, by year. Incumbent polarization has grown in step with the candidate supply. *Note*: Candidate ideology measured by static CFscores residualized by congressional district.

or, as I call them, new candidates (both challengers and open-seat candidates). Candidate ideologies, again measured by the CFScores scaling methodology, are first residualized by district so that the resulting calculations reveal candidate divergence and not sorting across districts.

The two lines track each other well ($r = 0.9$). As incumbent polarization has risen, so too has the ideological polarization of new candidates for the House. Incumbent polarization is also consistently below that of new candidate polarization. The results in chapter 3 provide the likely explanation for this fact. Voters tend to select more-moderate candidates from among the pool—thus producing Democratic and Republican incumbents who are closer together, on average, than the overall candidate pools. Nonetheless, incumbent polarization remains high. The candidate supply does not give voters the opportunity to shrink the difference between the candidates of the two parties further.

Voters Can Select Moderates but Cannot Force Candidates to Move to the Middle

The simulation and data I just presented offer a clear view of how this book will think about elections and polarization—a view that is at odds with much of the literature on polarization. In my view, voters are presented with candidates of varying ideologies, they choose some for office, and the ideologies of the winning candidates determine the degree of legislative polarization. But what if candidates moderate their positions after winning office? If candidates moderate in office, then electing more-extreme candidates does not necessarily create legislative polarization, because extreme candidates can become moderate incumbents.

This possibility is at the heart of the so-called median voter theorem, as encapsulated in the Downsian model (Downs 1957). Downs's influential theory predicts that candidates will converge, offering the positions that the median voter prefers in order to secure a majority of votes. As a result, it is a votercentric model of the political process; the precise identities of candidates do not matter because any candidate can choose any position. The Downsian logic underpins much of the work on polarization—it provides the theoretical logic for why voter preferences might imply something about the behavior of representatives and for why the behavior of representatives might reflect something about voter preferences.

However, a large body of work documents the failure of Downsian convergence in American elections. McCarty, Poole, and Rosenthal (2009, abstract) find that "congressional polarization is primarily a function of the differences in how Democrats and Republicans represent the same districts rather than a function of which districts each party represents or the distribution of constituency preferences." Ansolabehere, Snyder, and Stewart (2001) find a marked gap in positions between Democrats and Republicans even when running for election in districts with the same underlying partisanship. David Lee, Moretti, and Butler (2004) use a regression discontinuity design to focus on districts where a Democratic or Republican candidate is "as-if" randomly assigned to hold office. Districts that quasi-randomly receive a Democrat see much more liberal roll-call voting from their representative than do the districts that receive the Republican incumbent, even though the underlying preferences of the two sets of districts are, on average, identical. Anthony Fowler and Hall (2017) extend this design, concluding that "elected officials do not adapt their roll-call voting to their districts' preferences over time, and that voters do not systematically respond by replacing incumbents" (abstract). Ideological divergence in U.S. elections is persistent.[4]

The failure of the Downsian model should perhaps not be surprising from a theoretical perspective. As Besley (2006, 32) explains, "The model assumes that citizens care about policies while politicians are infinitely pliable—adopting any position to get elected. But if politicians have even a little preference for policies then they will have an incentive to renege after the election." This credibility problem is explored in depth by Alesina (1988).

More generally, we think of voters having two tools with which to influence ideological representation: (1) they can select candidates of particular ideological bents, and (2) they can pressure candidates into changing their positions (Fearon 1999). The evidence I just reviewed suggests that voters have little power to induce candidates to alter their platforms. As Fearon (1999, 76) sums up, "a number of empirical observations suggest that voters think about elections more in terms of selection than as sanctioning mechanisms to influence future incumbents." David Lee, Moretti, and Butler (2004, 849–50) conclude likewise, that "voters do not influence policy choices as much as they are presented with choices." Influenced by this logic, a recent body of literature in political economy places new emphasis on who become candidates and on how elections select among candidate types (e.g., Besley and Reynal-Querol 2011; Besley et al. 2017; Dal Bó et al. 2017). However, these works are primarily about competence rather than ideology. If, as the literature on candidate positioning suggests, candidates have relatively fixed ideological types, then voters' main chance to influence the ideological composition of their legislatures is to select candidates of particular ideologies.

Consistent with this general claim about candidate selection, classic work in American politics shows that candidates generally have fixed ideological positions over the length of their careers. Poole and Rosenthal (2000) use the entire set of roll-call votes in Congress to scale legislators from liberal to conservative. The resulting scalings offer a sense of which legislators tend to vote in which directions on bills that come up for consideration on the floor of the House or Senate. Most, but not all, members serve for more than one term, and so the authors can assess whether members' ideologies seem to change over time. Poole and Rosenthal conclude, "We find remarkable and increasing stability. . . . Members of Congress come to Washington with a staked-out position on the continuum, and then, largely die 'with their ideological boots on'" (2000, 8).

For the purposes of this book, I will think of candidates as mainly being of a fixed type, based on the accumulated evidence in favor of this claim. I am not claiming, nor do I need to assume, that candidates are entirely rigid; of course, there are instances in which candidates change their minds on specific issues. Genuine changes in preference, cynical flip-flops due to political pressures, and corruption all abound in American politics. But the overall ideological views of candidates are less mobile than many people think. The more rigid the candidate positions are, the more important candidate selection will be for understanding polarization. The framework of candidate types justifies a focus on who runs for office. In a world where candidate platforms are not altogether fluid, the strategic interaction between candidates and voters depends on who runs, and not just on how strategic candidates adjust their ideological platforms.

Why Devaluing Office Discourages Moderates from Running

As we have just seen, the U.S. House is polarized in part because of who runs for office. It is impossible for our legislatures to be populated with moderates if no moderates run for office, and incumbents do not generally moderate their positions after winning election. To understand polarization, therefore, and to identify ways we might reduce it in the future, we need to understand why some people choose to run for office and others do not. The remainder of this chapter is devoted to laying out a theoretical argument for why higher costs and lower benefits of running for office deter moderates, making the candidate pool more polarized.

A Thought Experiment

The theory is best introduced through a thought experiment. Imagine two citizens, Alice and Bob, considering running for the U.S. House. For concreteness, let's suppose Alice and Bob are registered Republicans, though this is not important for conveying any of the ideas. And let's suppose the Democratic candidate in their district is already well known (there is going to be an uncontested primary for the Democrats, let's say) and is not an incumbent.

Alice is a so-called moderate Republican, by which I mean that her views are not as far right as Bob's are relative to her potential constituents. A business executive, Alice supports what might generally be called "free-market" principles. This view includes broad support for policies that reduce tariffs and generally encourage free trade, as well as support for lowering corporate and individual income taxes. To accomplish these goals, Alice is willing to have the country run a deficit, which she believes to be sound policy. Alice opposes raises in the minimum wage and does not believe the government should be involved in dictating employer decisions related to, for example, unequal pay between men and women. On

the other hand, she differs from some of her fellow Republicans in holding what might be called socially liberal views on such issues as abortion
(she is prochoice) and gay marriage (which she supports). Though she is
ambivalent about general immigration policy, as a hirer of people with
advanced degrees, she strongly supports the expansion of H1-B visas for
highly skilled workers.

Bob, a small-business owner, is a hard-core member of the Tea Party.
He opposes the bulk of government spending. Bob agrees with Alice on
some of her "free-market"-oriented policies, but he believes that the debt
ceiling should never be raised under any circumstance. He believes that
the government should use military force to remove illegal immigrants
from the United States, and he believes that a significant military presence should be deployed along the U.S.–Mexico border to deter future illegal immigrants.

Alice and Bob's potential Democratic opponent—let's call her Claudia—
holds relatively mainstream Democratic views on all these issues, meaning that she displays broader support for redistributive programs, often at
odds with "free-market" principles (though not necessarily free trade),
strong support for gay marriage and for prochoice policy, and strong support for immigration amnesty and a variety of proimmigration policies.

Alice and Bob each sit down with their respective families to discuss
the decision to run for office. First, they consider the personal aspects of
the decision. How will their families navigate the scrutiny and stress of
a round-the-clock campaign? Running for office is no picnic, they know.
They each mull over their past. Is there anything an opponent could seize
on and, fairly or unfairly, use against them?

They worry, too, about the toll the long hours of a campaign will take
on their respective families. Running for office will mean long days of
making endless phone calls to potential donors, attending bland break-
fast events, making repetitive speeches, shaking hands, giving interviews,
and worrying constantly about how any tiny misstatement might balloon
into controversy. Somewhere in between these duties, Alice and Bob are
expected to find time to (we hope) study at least some of the policy issues
they're expected to hold forth on, not to mention do research on each other's campaigns, the state of the economy, current events, the president's
schedule and activities, and more. It is a 24/7 job. Alice and Bob will essentially not see their families until the campaign is over.

They also consider something more prosaic: their financial situations.
Can they and their families *afford* to run for office? Doing so requires

quitting, or at least taking a long leave of absence from, their respective jobs. If they win office, they must neglect their former jobs for even longer; if they lose, they may each be able to return to their jobs, but with a six-month backlog of work and ill will to make up for. In the meantime, debts will pile up, not just related to the campaign itself but simply because their families' expenses will continue unabated while they campaign for office.

Next, they and their families each discuss the feasibility of their respective campaigns. Will they be taken seriously, or will they embarrass themselves? Can they raise enough money quickly enough to become viable candidates? Will they get support from local party members, politically active business members, and the other local elites who involve themselves in the primary? Of course, they are not making these choices in a vacuum, and each has been contacted by various recruiters, but Alice and Bob are not sure how much these recruiters can deliver them electorally.

Then, they discuss the pluses and minuses of actually being a member of Congress. On the one hand, representing their district in Congress sounds like an honor, a prize worth fighting for. More selfishly, both Alice and Bob suspect that it could be a helpful springboard for their respective careers, since former members of Congress must get at least some benefit in terms of name recognition, opportunities to work as lobbyists, and so forth. On the other hand, they are both realistic about what a job in the House entails. Gridlock and polarization mean that they may have few opportunities to legislate. The party-oriented structure of the House means that they will be beholden at all turns to their party's leader, either the Speaker of the House or the House minority leader. They will be expected to spend most of their time "dialing for dollars," and they will have to fly back and forth to Washington, DC, every week. For all of these burdens, both Alice and Bob—as highly accomplished businesspeople— would be taking more than a 50 percent pay cut to serve in the House.

Finally, they talk about what their candidacies might mean for the country. Bob is forceful in his belief that Claudia *cannot* be allowed to represent their district. Her views are anathema to Bob and, in his view, borderline treasonous. If he does not run, Bob realizes, he may have to endure two years—and probably many more, given the incumbency advantage the winner will receive—of Claudia's left-wing representation. The thought is unbearable. Not surprisingly, taking it all in, Bob decides he has no choice but to run for office.

Though no fan of Claudia's platform, Alice is far more ambivalent than Bob. True, she finds Claudia's economic policies unwise and downright damaging to her business prospects. But others of Claudia's positions are not so far from her own. Although on net she might marginally prefer Bob to Claudia, neither seems particularly close or far from her own ideals. Given this ambivalence, and the daunting prospect of running a full-bore campaign, Alice decides to sit this one out.

It is this final difference—the way Alice and Bob, respectively, consider the ideological gains and losses of holding versus not holding office—that separate them. They face the same costs of running. In this story, they must raise the same amounts of money, make the same number of phone calls to the same number of people, endure the same levels of scrutiny, all for the same potential office—but they do not face the same ideological costs of not running. If Bob does not run, he might get stuck with Claudia, whom he finds completely, utterly objectionable. But if Alice stays out, she is merely displeased, not apoplectic, about the winner's platform. Alice's location toward the middle of the ideological spectrum makes her fear the specter of sitting out less.

Notice, too, that I have said nothing explicitly psychological about either Bob or Alice. It is not that Bob holds the views he holds more strongly than Alice's holds hers (though I can easily imagine that would be the case). It is not that Bob enjoys the soapbox that candidacy will give him more than would Alice (though I can easily imagine that would be the case, too). The only difference as I have told the story is that Bob is much farther from Claudia, ideologically, than Alice is from Claudia.

Imagine, now, that we took away many of the things that make running so hard. Imagine Alice and Bob could run without having to fundraise for six hours a day and without worrying about having to explain the contents of an irrelevant college essay written twenty-five years earlier. What would change? From Bob's perspective, while he would be happy to forgo these burdens, it would not change his decision. He had already decided to run even when things were harder; he is likely to continue to do so now that it's easier. But Alice might well switch from not running to running. Before, she chose not to run because not running was not so bad for her, ideologically, which made running not worth the modest benefits. But if running is easy, those more modest benefits might become worth it.

Formalizing the Thought Experiment

Now that I have laid out the thought experiment in words, I can formalize it a bit to clarify how it works. Figure 1.4 depicts the setup, as I described

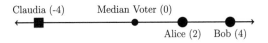

FIGURE 1.4. Alice and Bob each decide whether or not to run for office. Because Alice is closest to the median voter, she is the most moderate of the three candidates shown. Ideological position is one of three key factors in the decision to run; the candidates must also each consider the benefits and costs of running.

it in the previous section. Each potential candidate is marked based on his or her ideological positions, using a single dimension of ideology. We take Claudia, the Democratic candidate, as given. She is shown on the left side of the graph. Alice is the more moderate of the two possible Republican candidates, located relatively close to the median voter; Bob is farther out to the right.

Let's suppose that Alice and Bob simultaneously make the decision to run or not to run. If Alice runs and Bob does not, she wins office for sure in this model, because she is the most moderate of the three candidates. We will assume that Bob wins office only if he runs and Alice does not (in figure 1.4, Bob and Claudia are equally distant from the median, so we will assume for now that ties are resolved in favor of the right-wing candidate in this hypothetical district). For simplicity, we will also assume for now that if both Alice and Bob run, so that there are three candidates in the race, Alice wins office (if you prefer more specifics, suppose either that the Republican primary voters are strategic, and so they nominate Alice because she will win the general election, or that there's a three-candidate race in the general election in which Alice captures the most votes). And let's further suppose that Alice's and Bob's payoffs depend on:

- The ideological distance between themselves and the winner;
- The value, b, of winning office; and
- The cost, c, of running for office.

Why do Alice and Bob care about the ideological distance between their own ideal points and the winner's? In theories about executive policymaking, this assumption is straightforward; since executives can take unilateral action, if Alice and Bob care about policy, they have reasons to care about the difference between their preferred policy and the one the executive implements. This link is less clear in a legislative context. A winning legislative candidate is only one legislator among many in the legislature; his or her opportunities to influence policy are somewhat muted, and he or she is rarely, if ever, pivotal when casting a roll-call vote. Nevertheless, there are good reasons to think Alice and Bob will still care. One of the main jobs of a legislator is to take a position on behalf of constituents (Mayhew 1974), and voters appear to care about specific issue positions that their legislators take regardless of whether their vote made the difference between a bill passing or failing (Ansolabehere and Jones 2010). Moreover, by drafting and amending bills, legislators may in fact influence the outcomes of ideological policies even when they are not pivotal. As such, it is reasonable to focus on a model in which the actors care about the ideal point of the winning candidate and wish for it to be as close to their own ideal points as possible.

To keep things as simple as possible, let's suppose that their overall payoffs are simply the sum of this ideal distance and the other two, nonideological factors (where c comes in as a negative number). Table 1.1 presents the payoffs for each possible scenario, considering whether Alice and Bob each choose to run or not run for office. Consider the top left cell of the table. Here, both Alice and Bob choose to run. Since Alice is more moderate, she wins office over Bob and Claudia in this hypothetical race. The numbers in parentheses indicate that Bob receives a payoff of $-2-c$; the ideological distance between the winner (Alice) and his own ideal point is 2, and he further pays the cost, c, of running for office. Alice receives a payoff of $b-c$; she wins office, and so captures the benefits b, and she gets to implement her preferred policy, so she has no ideological loss—but she also pays the costs of running. The other three cells' payoffs are computed using the same logic.

Clearly, what Alice and Bob decide will matter on the precise values for b and c; that is, on the net benefits of winning office. Rather than look through the algebra from this generic table, we can explore this relationship through a few specific examples. In table 1.2, we first suppose that $b = 0$ and

TABLE 1.1 **Alice and Bob's Decision to Run Depends on Costs and Benefits**

		Alice	
		Run	Don't Run
Bob	Run	$(-2-c, b-c)$	$(b-c, -2)$
	Don't Run	$(-2, b-c)$	$(-8, -6)$

TABLE 1.2 **When Costs Are High, Bob Runs but Alice Doesn't**

		Alice	
		Run	Don't Run
Bob	Run	(−9, −7)	(−7, −2)
	Don't Run	(−2, −7)	(−8, −6)

$c = 7$, so that the net benefits of office are equal to −7. In this scenario, running for office is very costly. What do Alice and Bob decide?

First, let's examine the decision from Alice's perspective. If Bob runs, Alice can either run, in which case she wins office and obtains a payoff of −7, or she can sit the race out, in which case she receives a payoff of −2. Because the net benefits of office are so low in this hypothetical scenario, if Bob runs, Alice clearly will not. Although Alice disagrees with Bob, her payoff when he is in office is only −2—that is, the cost she pays for the ideological dissonance between herself and Bob isn't so much that it makes her want to bear the high costs of running. If Bob doesn't run, Alice now faces the risk of Claudia, who's farther from her than Bob is, winning office instead. Even in this case, though, the costs of running are so high that she would rather sit out and let Claudia win, preferring the −6 payoff from the ideological distance between herself and Claudia, the winner, to the −7 payoff from running and winning but paying the costs of running.

Since the payoffs are set up such that Alice always chooses not to run, we can now examine Bob's decision, fixing Alice's choice as "Don't Run." The decision is different for Bob than for Alice. If he runs, he has to pay the high cost to be a candidate, but he also wins and gets to implement his preferred ideological position. If he doesn't run, he suffers a massive cost from the fact that he is so far, ideologically, from Claudia. The extra distance between Bob and Claudia, versus between Alice and Claudia, makes all the difference. Unlike Alice, Bob chooses to run in this hypothetical scenario. *The high costs of running deter Alice but not Bob because Bob's extreme views make him more reluctant to accept Claudia as his representative.*

Now suppose that we raise the benefits of office or, equivalently, lower the costs of running—so that the net benefits of office go up. In particular, let's suppose that $c = 1$ and $b = 0$, so that $b − c = −1$ instead of −7 as before. Table 1.3 shows the resulting payoffs. The situation changes. Now Alice has a dominant strategy of "Run" because no matter what Bob decides, Alice always gets a higher payoff by running and holding office than by sitting out.

TABLE 1.3 **When Costs Are Low, Alice Runs and Wins**

		Alice	
		Run	Don't Run
Bob	Run	(−3, −1)	(−1, −2)
	Don't Run	(−2, −1)	(−8, −6)

This is because the net benefits, at −1, are now greater than the ideological cost of letting Bob win, which is a cost of −2. When the costs of running are low enough, or the benefits are high enough, Alice, the moderate, will run for office.

What I have just laid out is a simplified version of what is called the "citizen-candidate model" (Besley and Coate 1997; Osborne and Slivinski 1996). In appendix 1, I go through the full model, and I establish the formal prediction that higher costs or lower benefits will produce more divergent equilibria.

The story I have laid out is highly stylized. Reality is much more complicated. Even in a simple, highly abstract game theoretic setup, the precise manner in which the story of Alice and Bob holds will be more complex. Nonetheless, the basic lesson will remain the same. The fact that people whose views are closer to the middle have less to lose by sitting out if they think more-extreme people are going to run will drive the ideological divergence of those who run in each party. And this phenomenon becomes all the stronger as running for office becomes harder or holding office become less attractive.

Summary: The Need to Understand Who Runs

Since 1980, American legislatures have polarized to an unprecedented extent. The consequences of this polarization could be problematic, but we still don't understand where this polarization has come from. In this chapter, I presented evidence that voters' choices over candidates, alone, explain relatively little of the polarization in American legislatures—even though most of the literature on polarization focuses on voters' preferences. Instead, as I argued, we need to look at who is running for office. As I showed, the set of people running for office has polarized along with the polarization in our legislatures. If we want to understand polarization, we need to understand who runs for office.

In the latter half of the chapter, I laid out a theoretical argument for how the costs of running for office and the benefits of holding office influence who runs. When costs are low or benefits are high (or both), I argued, more moderate people will be willing to run for office. When costs are high or benefits are low (or both), the candidate pool is predicted to become more extreme. The remainder of the book applies this theoretical argument to the U.S. House and offers evidence for its validity.

CHAPTER TWO

A Framework for Studying Elections and Ideology

The key data is this, and it's important to re-emphasize if only to shut up the useless, overpaid political consultants who idiotically babble about "moving to the center" or "compromising with the other side." . . . What matters is turning out our voters. That's it. The Democrats win when we fire up and turn out our base.—Blog post on Daily Kos

Democrats cannot win elections without capturing the votes of independent-minded swing voters.—Commentary in the *Wall Street Journal*

Do more-moderate candidates outperform more-extreme candidates in U.S. elections? Members of both parties debate this question passionately as they weigh which primary candidates to support as their standard-bearers. It is also a crucial question for this book. My argument that the rise in legislative polarization is due, in part, to a decrease in the propensity of moderate citizens to run for office relies on the idea that more-moderate candidates would win office if they ran.

It is perhaps unsurprising that more-moderate people tend to argue that more-moderate candidates do better, while those farther on the left and right argue the opposite. What is more surprising is that political scientists are themselves deeply divided on the question of candidate ideology and electoral performance, despite more than fifty years spent studying the issue empirically.

The dominant approach to studying elections and ideology in political science uses survey evidence to explore how uninformed and partisan voters are (e.g., Campbell et al. 1960; Converse 1964; Kinder and Kalmoe 2017; Lenz 2012; Miller and Stokes 1963).[1] Many observers infer from these findings that there cannot be an advantage for moderate candidates because voters don't know who is moderate and vote along strictly partisan lines. In perhaps the most forceful version of this argument, Achen and Bartels (2016a, 311–12) assert that more-moderate candidates are not advantaged because "election outcomes are essentially random choices among the available parties."

On the other hand, research that combines election data with measures of candidate ideology consistently finds an electoral advantage for moderate candidates (e.g., Ansolabehere, Snyder, and Stewart 2001; Canes-Wrone, Brady, and Cogan 2002; Erikson 1971; Erikson and Wright 2000; Hall 2015; Hall and Thompson forthcoming). Why do these two literatures reach differing conclusions, and what should we conclude?

In this chapter, I argue that much of this divide goes away after we clarify our empirical goals. As I explain, for the specific question of where legislative polarization comes from, and whether it has to do with more-extreme candidates winning elections over more-moderate candidates, we want to answer the question of whether or not electorates favor more-moderate candidates, *regardless of why they do so*. I call this the question of *electoral selection*: do U.S. House electorates favor more-moderate candidates? This is not the question implicit in most of the survey-based literature, which instead asks whether individual voters are aware of particular candidate positions and whether changes in these candidate positions would alter their view of the candidate.

The first part of the chapter explains why we want to study electoral selection and why it is different from the question of whether changing positions would boost a candidate's vote share. To help explain this point, I offer a thought experiment about a hypothetical world in which all moderate candidates are tall, all extreme candidates are short, and voters vote purely based on candidate height. In this world, electoral choices will not polarize the legislature because voters will consistently choose moderates for office. Although they do not elect the moderate candidates *because* they are moderate—rather, they elect them because they are tall—their choices have ideological consequences for the legislature nonetheless. If we were somehow able to separate out the effect of ideological positioning from the effect of candidate height, we would find no effect of ideology—and we would mistakenly conclude that electorates do not favor more-moderate candidates.

Identifying the correct question to ask is only half the battle, though. Studying electoral selection empirically is challenging, and it is only because of recent advances in technology and statistics that we are able to leverage large-scale data to successfully address the challenges.

The key difficulty is that, to study electoral selection, we need to compare the ideology of winning candidates to the ideology of everyone who runs for office, including losing candidates. Most techniques to measure candidate ideology rely on using roll-call votes, but only winners—incumbents—cast roll-call votes. I solve this problem by using estimates of candidate ideology based on campaign-contribution data. I discuss how these techniques work, and I address concerns about their validity. Although important journal articles have identified particular issues with CFscores (Hill and Huber 2017; Tausanovitch and Warshaw 2017), there are many ways to use contributions to scale candidates. Each way is useful, and we can use the full constellation of available scalings to make sure results are not driven by any particular flaw of any particular measure. By doing so, we can be confident that the results do not confuse strategic donation for ideology and do not confuse partisanship for ideology.

Even with a valid measure of candidate ideology, there remains another major empirical obstacle, which is the need to hold each district's underlying ideological preferences fixed. Accordingly, I review the assumptions deployed in existing research to attempt to achieve this goal. To add to the existing literature, I then describe my quasi-experimental design (from Hall 2015), which focuses on close U.S. House primary elections between more-moderate and more-extreme candidates. This approach allows us to estimate how elections favor candidates of varying ideology with different and perhaps weaker assumptions than existing work.

Having offered this methodological overview, chapter 3 applies it to election data, showing that U.S. House elections favor moderate candidates, on average. I conclude that U.S. House electorates are constrained by the candidate pool; they prefer more-moderate candidates, on average, but are often forced to elect more-extreme candidates because so few moderates run for office.

Electoral Selection versus Effects of Candidate Positioning

This book's argument is that who runs for office helps determine the level of ideological polarization in the legislature. My claim is that when more-moderate people run for office, they win election at high rates and the polarization of the legislature is lower. Evaluating this claim requires testing whether or not electorates select more-moderate candidates for office. If electorates tend to select moderates, then we can suspect that who runs for office in the first place matters; on the other hand, if electorates select extremists, then we might suspect that who runs is less important because moderates would not win office even if they ran.

Electoral selection is distinct from the question of *how* voters make their individual choices in elections. A long tradition in the study of political behavior, focusing on surveys, sees voters as largely uninformed and "ideologically innocent" (for a review, see Kinder and Kalmoe 2017). Recent work in this tradition has declared voters to be "tribal partisans" who support their parties' candidates regardless of ideological positions (e.g., Achen and Bartels 2016a). Bolstering this view, survey research suggests that, to the extent that voters have policy views, they mostly mimic those handed down by elites and party leaders (Lenz 2012). These ideas have caught fire among pundits as well. Vox's Ezra Klein (2017) declares, "Party trumps ideology." Talking about Republican voters, he claims that their Republicanism is "based more on group attachments . . . than it is on ideology."

These views have led many observers to conclude that moderate candidates do not possess an electoral advantage. This logic is summarized concisely by Eric Levitz (2017) in an essay entitled "Democrats Can Abandon the Center—Because the Center Doesn't Exist": "In sum: Almost no one in the United States has uniformly 'moderate' policy views; on individual issues, the electorate's consensus positions are often ideologically 'extreme'; partisan voters are typically drawn to one party over the other for reasons of group identity rather than personal ideology; such voters take their ideological cues, on most policies, from party elites; and many voters don't know enough about each party's policy commitments to vote on the basis of their ideological preferences, even if they wanted to." Here is the key point. Whether specific claims about voters being uninformed, ideologically incoherent partisans are true—for a more skeptical take, see Fowler (2018)—they do not speak to the question of electoral selection, which is our focus here. That is, *surveys of individual voters' issue positions and partisanship cannot tell us whether or not moderate candidates possess an electoral advantage in U.S. House elections*.

An analogy may help make this point clear. Suppose a researcher surveys a set of people considering purchasing smartphones, asking them specific questions about the differing features that iPhones and LG phones have. The survey reveals that the respondents know next to nothing about these details: they cannot say which phone has more memory, a larger screen, or longer battery life. Based on these results, a naive observer concludes that consumers can't possibly prefer one smartphone brand over another, because they know nothing about their phones' respective features.

In reality, Apple sells far more smartphones in the United States than LG Electronics does. The naive observer misinterprets the survey because questions about specific characteristics cannot speak to the question of which phones consumers purchase in practice. It's probably true that consumers know very little about the technical details of different smartphones, but we cannot conclude from this that one smartphone can't be advantaged over another. Consumers may prefer iPhones for many other reasons not captured by the particular set of questions the researcher chose to ask. Moreover, in the real world, consumers see advertising, get advice, consider prices, and are in general bombarded with all kinds of stimuli not captured in such a survey. Eliciting their views over specific smartphone features is not sufficient for understanding aggregate purchasing behavior in the real world. That does not mean the survey is not useful; it just means that, if the naive observer wants to know which phone is more popular, he or she should examine data on smartphone sales by brand, rather than surveys about consumer preferences.

Just like in this analogy, survey evidence that voters are partisan and don't know much about candidates—which may be valuable for many reasons—is ill suited for studying electoral selection. Surveys may not ask voters exactly the right set of issue positions necessary to figure out their overall opinion of candidates. Moreover, electorates might select moderate candidates even if voters know little about positions, are rigidly partisan, or have incoherent policy views. Even the most extreme accounts of the tribal partisanship hypothesis suggest that voters may have multiple identities and that campaigns could "activate" these different identities. If moderate candidates are better able to activate certain identities, perhaps because of how they run their campaigns, or because of support they get from their parties, then electorates could advantage moderate candidates even in this hypothetical world of rigid partisanship.

In a journal article coauthored with Daniel Thompson, I make particularly clear the distinction between whom elections choose in the aggregate and how individual voters behave (Hall and Thompson forthcoming). We show that extremist nominees in competitive primaries for the U.S. House do worse than more-moderate nominees, on average, because they affect the composition of turnout in the general election. When a party nominates an extremist in a U.S. House primary, more voters in the other party turn out in the general election, on average. The findings show that voters can make ideological choices even without casting an ideologically informed vote, and even if they are mostly rigid partisans, because their decision to turn out is linked to whether a more moderate or a more extreme candidate is nominated.

In steering away from the behavior of individual voters, our focus on electoral selection also steers away from studying the hypothetical effects of candidate positioning. In chapter 1, I quoted an op-ed by Achen and Bartels which asserted that "the electoral penalty for candidates *taking* extreme positions is quite modest because voters in the political center do not reliably support the candidates closest to them on the issues" (2016b, emphasis mine). Implicitly, this statement concerns a causal effect of candidate positioning—it implies that candidates can choose, or "take," a variety of positions, and that the causal effect of them taking more-extreme positions on election outcomes is close to zero. Work that formally randomizes hypothetical candidates' positions in survey vignettes makes this goal especially explicit (e.g., Ahler and Broockman 2016; Gerber, Gooch, and Huber 2017; Harbridge and Malhotra 2011; Tomz and Van Houweling 2008).

These causal effects are completely different from electoral selection, and one cannot be used to estimate the other. Suppose—as an extreme hypothetical!—that all moderate candidates are tall and all extreme candidates are short, and that voters know nothing about candidate positions and vote purely based on height, preferring taller candidates to shorter ones. Now let's suppose that we as researchers ask the question: do moderate candidates make it into office? In this hypothetical, the answer will be yes, not because taking more-moderate positions "causes" a candidate to do better but rather because only moderate candidates are tall, and voters only vote for tall candidates.

In answering this question, we will learn whether more-extreme candidates are winning races and making it into the legislature, which teaches us about the roots of legislative polarization. In particular, in this hypothetical scenario, we would learn that electoral choices are not driving legislative polarization because voters are voting for more moderate candidates. We will not necessarily observe the mechanism by which they win races (in this case, their height), but we will observe the ideological consequences. That is, *elections have ideological consequences for the legislature even if the mechanism by which voters choose whom to vote for is not ideological*.

Measuring Candidate Ideology with Campaign Contributions

Clarifying our empirical goals is insufficient for solving the problem of how to study electoral selection; we must now confront a fundamental empirical challenge that has prevented most scholars from studying electoral selection in the context of candidate ideology until recently.

The most effective way to study electoral selection is to compare the ideological positions of candidates who are elected to office to those who are not. Are the winners more moderate than the losers? If so, we have evidence that U.S. House electorates favor more-moderate candidates. Answering the question requires being able to measure the ideology of both winners and losers, and this has been the key problem for political scientists. Whereas we have effective ways to measure the ideological positions of winners, through the roll-call votes they cast in the legislature, we have lacked an analogous technique for losers, who never cast roll-call votes. Although some particularly creative work has tried to solve this issue, either by studying challengers who go on to be incumbents who cast roll-call votes later or by using surveys that candidates for the House filled out at some point (Ansolabehere, Snyder, and Stewart 2001), the resulting analyses are limited in scope.

Fortunately, recent methodological work solves this problem on a much broader scale. I will focus primarily on three main measures of candidate ideology. The first, which is the most commonly used, comes from Bonica (2014) and is called CFScores, downloaded online from the Database on Ideology, Money in Politics, and Elections (DIME). CFScores offer estimates of ideology for 24,123 candidates for the U.S. House from 1980 through 2014. To make sure my conclusions are not driven by the use of CFScores, I will also show the robustness of my conclusions to two other scaling techniques which rely on different assumptions about the contribution process. The first alternate measure is the DW-DIME score, which uses machine learning to predict candidate roll-call ideology based on their contributions. The second alternate measure comes from work I did with James M. Snyder Jr. (2015a), which uses a simpler technique to impute candidate ideology based on the roll-call ideologies of incumbents to whom their donors also donated in the past.

All of these methods try to extract an indication of candidate ideology using the mix of campaign contributions that candidates, both winners and losers, receive from donors. To understand the idea, think about a new candidate running for office. We don't know much about her ideological positions because she has yet to serve in the legislature. But she has started to make speeches, to offer issue positions, and, most important, to raise money for her campaign. If we see that she receives most of her donations from donors who typically support, say, far left-wing candidates, then we have good reason to think that she, too, is probably a left-wing candidate. In principle, we could extract all of her position statements from her speeches, conversations, and so forth to measure her overall ideological positions directly, but this is not practical. The sheer amount of data would require decades of collection, processing, and interpretation. Instead, CFScores let the donors do that work for us; they are a useful indication of what the candidate's positions are, precisely because donors pay special attention to the political process, tend to know something about the candidates to whom they donate, and tend to care about candidates' positions.

Contribution-Based Scalings Pass Basic Validity Tests

The first criterion by which to evaluate contribution-based scalings is this: do they measure actual candidate ideology? In brief, the answer is yes. I will not dwell on this issue, only because it has been dealt with in much greater detail by Bonica (2013), who offers a variety of findings, including the following:

1. CFScores correlate highly with roll-call based measures of ideology for sitting incumbents, even within party.
2. CFScores accurately classify incumbents' roll-call votes without conditioning on their roll-call-based measures of ideology.
3. CFScores appear to extract a meaningful indicator of ideology even for cases where the correlation with roll-call-based measures is weaker.

These findings are also true for DW-DIME and for Hall-Snyder scores. Although correlation with DW-NOMINATE is not the be-all and end-all of contribution-based scaling (see discussion that follows), DW-DIME and Hall-Snyder both correlate with NOMINATE quite highly (in the case of DW-DIME, extremely highly, since it is designed to do so.)[2]

Strategic Donating as Threat to Contribution-Based Scalings

The main criticism leveled at all contribution-based scaling techniques is that money is often given strategically. We have ample evidence, both statistical and qualitative, that interest groups donate to incumbents in exchange for political access (e.g., Fouirnaies and Hall 2014, 2018; Grimmer and Powell 2016; James Snyder 1992). Donations given in this manner will not reveal ideology. Moreover, because interest groups that are strategic will likely seek access to members of both parties, these donors may appear moderate when in fact they are simply nonideological. There is no doubt

that this behavior occurs. However, it does not raise nearly as large a problem for the money-based scalings as one might think, because the reality is
that such interest groups comprise a relatively small amount of the entire
donor pool. More than 50 percent of all contributions in federal elections
are made by individuals (Ansolabehere, de Figueiredo, and Snyder 2003;
Barber, Canes-Wrone, and Thrower 2017). Individuals, unlike groups, are
generally thought to be nonstrategic in their contributions, so that their
money credibly reveals with which candidates they align. Barber, Canes-
Wrone, and Thrower (2017), for a recent example, show that individual donors tend to support candidates who agree with them ideologically. This is
the main reason the scalings seem to work so well. Indeed, money-based
scalings that throw out interest-group contributions and use only individual
contributions are extremely highly correlated with those that use all donations.[3] Moreover, Bonica (2014) performs a series of analyses to compare
ideological and nonideological models of giving, finding further support
for the notion that CFScores reflect ideology and not strategic donating.

The Hall-Snyder scaling also attacks this problem head-on. To avoid
it, Hall-Snyder only scales candidates based on the contributions they receive in primary elections *before they become incumbents*, therefore sev-
ering the link between incumbency and access-seeking donations. This is
perhaps the simplest and most direct way to make absolutely certain that
strategic donating cannot drive the results.

Do Contribution-Based Scalings Detect More Than Partisanship?

Another potential issue with contribution-based scalings is that, under
some techniques, they do not correlate well with DW-NOMINATE, the
predominant approach to measuring incumbent ideology based on roll-
call votes, when making within-party comparisons for nonincumbent candidates (Tausanovitch and Warshaw 2017). In the worst case of all, Bonica
(2013) shows that, among Democratic candidates challenging Republican
incumbents in the U.S. House, the correlation between CFScores and
DW-NOMINATE scores (for the set of open-seat Democratic candidates
who go on to serve in the legislature) is only 0.2. The correlation is better
for Republican challengers facing Democratic incumbents (0.49), and for
open-seat candidates of both parties (0.4), but still relatively weak. How
should we think about this important issue?

The DW-DIME scalings developed by Bonica (forthcoming) address
the issue that CFScores do not correlate well with DW-NOMINATE
within party by constructing a measure explicitly meant to maximize this

within-party correlation. The scalings use machine learning to figure out which donors are most predictive of DW-NOMINATE scalings and then to use these donors to construct scores for every candidate. The resulting scalings correlate incredibly highly with DW-NOMINATE within party. In addition, because the method relies on identifying informative donors, we can further validate the method by looking at who these informative donors are. Bonica (forthcoming) concludes that the most informative donors for the scalings are not donors who split their money between the parties, but instead are single-party donors who support ideologically unusual factions of their parties. Table 3 in the work by Bonica (forthcoming) shows that the two most informative donors are the Blue Dog Democrats (100 percent of donations in 2016 to Democrats, according to OpenSecrets) and the Citizens Against Government Waste (100 percent of donations in 2016 to Republicans, according to OpenSecrets.)

More conceptually, as Bonica (2013, forthcoming) discusses, there is no sense in which DW-NOMINATE is the ground truth. No scaling technique can isolate ideology, since it is such a complicated object with different meanings in different contexts. Roll-call votes indicate one important aspect of the concept, the part related to the incumbent's formal behavior in the legislature.[4] Sometimes, as when we are specifically studying roll-call votes—one of the most important representative acts a legislator performs—it makes sense to focus on measures that explicitly attempt to predict roll-call votes for candidates who have not cast them. In other contexts, the goal might not be specifically to predict roll-call votes. When voters, elites, and the media consider the ideology of potential representatives, they may consider a variety of factors. How will a potential candidate shape legislation? What issues will he or she prioritize? Whose voices will he or she listen to? These activities include roll-call voting, but also many other items that are distinct from roll-call voting. The mix of campaign contributions a candidate receives may tell us something about who is extreme and who is moderate—in the precise sense of what kinds of donors the candidate's portfolio is weighted toward—that is valuable and somewhat distinct from roll-call voting. This is why it is not clear that the goal of contribution-based scalings should be to perfectly recover the NOMINATE scaling. This is clearest to us when considering the Hall-Snyder scalings. As described earlier, these scalings convey substantive information whether or not they correlate with NOMINATE scores. It is coherent to talk about an extremist—a candidate who raises most of his or her money from donors who tend to donate to extreme members of the legislature—in the context of these scalings.[5]

Are Contribution-Based Scalings Comparable over Time?

A final concern with contribution-based scalings is that they may reflect changes in the behavior and opinions of donors over time, instead of changes in the ideology of the candidate pool over time. Bonica (2014) tackles this issue head-on, showing that the scores exhibit significant stability over time. In particular, he estimates separate scalings for each candidate in each time period while holding donor ideal points constant, and then compares these scalings to the CFScore scaling, finding that they are very similar. In fact, Bonica finds that CFScores are more stable even than DW-NOMINATE scores, which, as I discussed in chapter 1, show that members of Congress have stable positions over time. It is not the case that changes in CFScores over time indicate changes in donor behavior. Moreover, similar arguments can be made for DW-DIME and Hall-Snyder scores, both of which are built off of DW-NOMINATE scores, which are explicitly created to be comparable over time.

The Range of Contribution-Based Scalings Addresses Major Concerns

In summary, although individual contribution-based scaling techniques have specific drawbacks—CFScores do not correlate well with roll-call based measures of incumbents within party, while DW-DIME could reflect in part strategic donations, and Hall-Snyder uses a simplistic statistical method—we can use all three of these techniques to make sure our conclusions are not driven by these specific flaws. The evidence that electorates prefer more-moderate candidates, as well as the evidence that the House is polarizing because of who runs for office, is strong under all possible scaling methods. Therefore, the conclusions of this book do not appear to be the result of strategic donating or partisanship; to the best we can tell, they reflect real, ideological phenomena.

Existing Evidence That Elections Favor Moderates

A central challenge to studying candidate ideology is that we do not know what each district's ideological preferences over candidates are. For the purposes of this methodological discussion, I will suppose that each district has an unobserved median voter whose ideology can be placed on a unidimensional scale. We know that candidates for U.S. House elections can be arrayed unidimensionally with considerable accuracy (e.g., Poole and Rosenthal 1985). The placement of the hypothetical median voter in the figures that follow should be thought of as describing the ideological positioning of the candidate the district would most prefer to elect. It need not be a direct statement about the ideological positioning of individual voters or survey respondents in the district.

Probably the best-known evidence that voters prefer more-moderate candidates, on average, comes from Canes-Wrone, Brady, and Cogan (2002). The authors compare incumbents who compile differing roll-call records and link their ideology to their electoral performance. In particular, their work defines a variable called "Roll-Call Ideological Extremism," which takes on higher values for members of the legislature whose roll-call record indicates they are farther into the wings of their respective parties.

The key obstacle to this measure, for our purposes, is that it does not immediately imply that a candidate is extreme *for his or her district.* Imagine two Democratic incumbents, one from a very liberal district in Massachusetts, the other from a more centrist district in Texas. The Massachusetts incumbent is likely to have a much more extreme roll-call record than the Texas one, but we cannot conclude from this evidence alone which one is farther from his or her district's unobserved, hypothetical median voter. It is entirely possible that it is the Texas incumbent who is farther away.

To tackle this issue, Canes-Wrone, Brady, and Cogan (2002) control for a proxy of district ideology—presidential vote share. Instead of making a raw comparison across members with more-extreme or less-extreme roll-call records, they make these comparisons only among districts that showed similar support for the Democratic presidential candidate. The hope is that such districts have similar ideological preferences and, therefore, that increases in roll-call extremism imply an increase in the distance from the unobserved median.

Figure 2.1 helps make the setup clear. The figure shows two hypothetical districts with the same unobserved median voter. In the first district, the Republican incumbent is farther to the right; in the second, the Republican incumbent is closer to the median. This is an ideal case. As long as the unobserved median is to the correct side—that is, to the left of Republican incumbents and to the right of Democratic ones—shifts in roll-call ideological extremism will accord with the Downsian notion of extremism perfectly (see Downs 1957).

The approach therefore requires two key assumptions. First, presidential vote share must be an effective means for holding fixed the unobserved

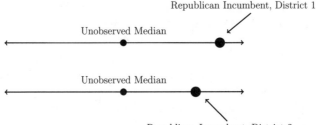

FIGURE 2.1. Studying candidate positions when median voter is unobserved but held constant. This approach assumes that presidential vote share is an effective means for holding fixed the unobserved median voter and that the unobserved median voter is to the correct side of the incumbents being studied—in this case, to the left of the two Republican candidates. In this figure, the incumbent in District 1 is farther from the median and thus shows a greater degree of ideological extremism based on roll-call votes.

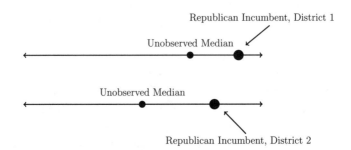

FIGURE 2.2. Studying candidate positions when median voter is unobserved and not held constant. In this scenario, because the position of the median voter is not the same across districts, the incumbent in District 1 is considered more extreme based on roll-call votes despite being *closer* to the median voter in that district than is the incumbent in District 2.

median voter; and second, the unobserved median voter must be to the proper side of the incumbents being studied. These are reasonable though not innocuous assumptions, and all studies will have to do something similar in order to make progress, empirically. How would the design be affected if these assumptions were violated?

A violation of the presidential vote share assumption could cause serious problems. Consider the situation presented in figure 2.2. Again, we compare Republican incumbents in two districts; this time, however, the unobserved median varies. Suppose that, despite this variation, the presidential vote share in the two districts is equal (perhaps because voters vote differently in presidential races, or because the median has changed in between a previous presidential election and the current congressional election, or for some other reason). The design is now biased. The incumbent in district 1 is considered more extreme based on roll-call votes even though this legislator is actually *closer* to the district's median voter than is the incumbent in district 2. Most likely, a problem like this would attenuate the association between moderation and electoral success, but it is possible that the bias could go in any direction.

Violations of the second assumption cause similar problems. In cases where the median is on the other side of the incumbent—in this case, farther to the right than the Republican—the definition of extreme again breaks down. Again, though, this adds error which should in general bias against finding an advantage for moderate candidates.

Ansolabehere, Snyder, and Stewart (2001) offer further evidence for the advantage of moderate candidates, using information about both candidates—incumbents and challengers, as well as open-seat candidates in some cases. The appendix to their work lays out the precise conditions under which we can link changes in ideological positions to proximity to the median voter. First, they hold fixed the district's ideology using presidential vote share, just as did Canes-Wrone, Brady, and Cogan (2002). Next, they also hold fixed the ideological distance between the Democratic and Republican candidates. In this framework, shifts in the *midpoint* between the two candidates have an unambiguous interpretation. A shift right in this midpoint *must* imply that the Republican candidate is worse off, spatially. Likewise, a shift left in the midpoint must imply that the Democratic candidate is worse off, spatially.

Figure 2.3 lays out this logic visually. In the first district, the Democratic candidate is closer to the unobserved median voter than the Republican candidate is. In the second district, the candidates have shifted left but the distance between them has stayed the same, and the unobserved median has not moved. This shift is unequivocally good for the Republican candidate in the spatial model. Regardless of whether the median voter is to the left of the Democratic candidate, in between them (as pictured), or to the right of the Republican, the shift left can only hurt the Democratic candidate relative to the Republican.

Ansolabehere, Snyder, and Stewart (2001) link observed shifts of this form to electoral outcomes, and they find that more-moderate candidates possess a significant electoral advantage. In performing these analyses, they use the midpoint technique to obviate the need to assume that the median

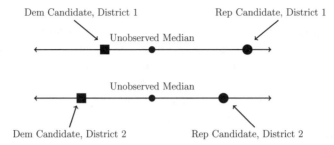

FIGURE 2.3. The midpoint approach for studying candidate positions when median voter is unobserved but held constant. This approach holds fixed not only the district's ideology, using presidential vote share, but also the ideological distance between the Democratic (squares) and Republican (larger circles) candidates, and thus it can focus on shifts in the midpoint between the two candidates. In District 1, the Democratic candidate is closer to the unobserved median voter than the Republican candidate is. The midpoint shift toward the left in District 2 moves the Democrat farther away from the median voter and brings the Republican closer.

voter is located in between the Democratic and Republican candidates. However, they still must assume that presidential vote share can hold the location of the unobserved median voter constant. Though I will not discuss them in detail, several other well-cited works employ similar evidence and come to similar conclusions (Burden 2004; Erikson 1971; Erikson and Wright 2000). Taken together, this literature strongly suggests that more-moderate candidates perform better in U.S. House elections. Nonetheless, some concerns may persist. I now turn to quasi-experimental design that relaxes the key assumptions from these studies.

The Primary-Election Regression Discontinuity Design

In this section, I lay out a quasi-experimental approach that, as chapter 3 will show, again finds a large electoral advantage to more-moderate candidates in the U.S. House. Randomized experiments solve issues of confounding variables because they ensure that treated and control units are otherwise alike, on average. Although we cannot run an experiment on U.S. House elections, we can take advantage of circumstances that approximate an experiment in which a more extreme or a more moderate candidate is nominated for the general election. The value of this quasi experiment is that it will allow us to hold districts' underlying preferences over candidates fixed, on average, without having to to employ the assumption that controlling for presidential vote share is sufficient.

Following my earlier work (Hall 2015), we study how U.S. House electorates choose candidates of varying ideologies using a quasi-experimental design focused on close primary elections. The logic, like that of other electoral regression discontinuity (RD) designs (e.g., D. Lee 2008), is as follows. In general, districts that choose to nominate more-extreme candidates for the general election will vary, systematically, from districts that choose to nominate more-moderate candidates. Most obviously, they are likely to be districts that prefer more-extreme candidates. We can account for these differences by focusing on very close primary elections where a more moderate or a more extreme candidate barely wins the nomination. The closer these primary elections are, the more random the outcome of the race is, and thus the more comparable the districts that nominate extremists will be to the districts that instead nominate more-moderate candidates.

The RD design relies on the assumption that there is no sorting at the discontinuity—that is, that in hypothetical tied races, there is no systematic difference in the districts that nominate a more moderate or more extreme candidate. Although researchers have raised doubts about this assumption in a particular set of U.S. House general elections (Caughey and Sekhon 2011; Snyder 2005), further research shows that the general assumption is sound (Eggers et al. 2015). Moreover, as I have shown elsewhere (Hall 2015; Hall and Thompson forthcoming), U.S. House primary elections show no evidence of violating the RD assumption.

The design starts by defining moderate versus extremist candidates based on their positions relative to one another. That is, without observing the district's median, I compare candidates competing with one another in a primary election. I focus on the two candidates in each contested primary race who receive the highest vote totals. For Democrats, the farther left candidate is called "extremist" and the farther right candidate is considered the "moderate"; while for Republicans, the farther right candidate is the "extremist" and the farther left the "moderate."

Figure 2.4 presents the research design. The top two diagrams show a hypothetical district holding two primary elections, one for the Democrats (on the left) and one for the Republicans (on the right). In each case we focus on the ideological positioning of the top two vote-getting primary candidates; hence, four candidates in total are shown. Focus first on the Democratic candidates in the top diagram. The leftmost candidate is defined as the extremist in this election by being farther to the left than the opponent, whom we call the moderate (even though even this candidate

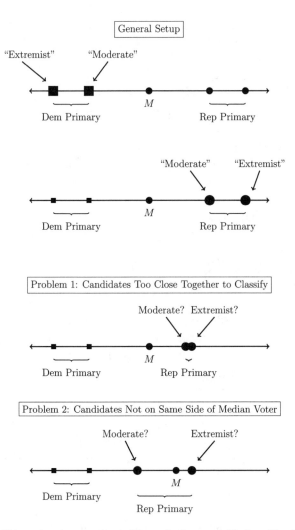

FIGURE 2.4. Using primaries to study candidate selection across ideology. The diagrams in this figure illustrate primary elections in a hypothetical district, where M represents the median voter. The top two Democratic candidates to the left of M (squares) and top two the Republican candidates to the right of M (circles) are shown labeled as "Extremist" or "Moderate," based on their ideological position in relation to the other candidate from their own party. Problems in this research design arise when the party's two candidates are too close together to classify or when they are not on the same side of the median voter.

is far removed from the median voter's position). Now consider the second diagram, focusing on the Republican candidates in the same district at the same time. Here, the definitions are reversed, in the sense that it is the rightmost candidate who is called the extremist and the less-farther-right candidate who is called the moderate. Again, these definitions are entirely relative to the district.

This is the ideal case for the research design, similar to the way in which Canes-Wrone, Brady, and Cogan (2002) hope for candidates to be on the correct side of the median voter in the district. Here, the key is that a party's primary candidates are arrayed all to the correct side of the median, allowing for coherent definitions of extremists versus moderates.

How can this design in figure 2.4 go awry? There are two major potential obstacles. The first, shown in the third diagram (labeled "Problem 1"), is that the candidates can be too close together. Here, the two Republican candidates are still to the correct side of the median, but they are estimated to have similar ideological positions. Which one is truly the moderate, then? This is a difficult question in two ways: first, it's hard to believe such small ideological differences could matter much; and second, since candidate positions are in fact measured with error, we cannot be confident we have even rank-ordered the two candidates correctly in a case like this.

To address the first issue, I focus (preliminarily) on races where the distance between the top two candidates is large. Specifically, in primary races with two major candidates, the race is tentatively identified as being between an extremist and a relatively moderate candidate if the difference between their estimated ideological positions using CFScores is at or above the median in the distribution of ideological distances between the top two candidates in all contested primary elections. These are therefore races between candidates who offer meaningfully different platforms within the umbrella of their party. Using a strong cutoff like this has two potential advantages. First, it may reduce the number of incorrect moderate or extremist labels caused by measurement error in the donor scores. Second, it ensures that we are focusing on strong comparisons in which the two primary candidates are starkly different.

The second issue, present also in Canes-Wrone, Brady, and Cogan (2002), is that there may be cases in which the party's candidates are not on the correct side of the median. Consider the fourth and final diagram in figure 2.4 (labeled "Problem 2"). In this case, the less-farther-right Republican candidate is actually to the left of the median voter, on the incorrect side, while the rightmost Republican candidate is to the right of the median voter, on the correct side, but closer to the median voter than the Republican opponent is. The procedure will still label the less-farther-right Republican candidate the moderate even though this candidate is farther away from the district's median voter than the one labeled extremist is. There is no obvious way to tackle this issue directly in the empirical design. Instead, we must think substantively about how likely we think it is to occur and, if it does occur, about how it will affect the results.

The first thing to say is that such a violation seems unlikely, in most cases. As the discussion in chapter 2 made clear, we know that candidates of the two parties tend to diverge, profoundly, even when running to serve the same voters. It would be difficult (though perhaps not impossible) to produce such a consistent divergence without the median voter located in between the two parties' candidates, which, in turn, would suggest that the two parties tend to "straddle" the median voter.[6]

Second, and perhaps more important, such violations would bias us away from finding a penalty to nominating more-extreme candidates. The more often we incorrectly label a moderate candidate extreme, and vice versa, the more noise we add to our treatment variable, and the more we thus attenuate the estimated effect of nominating an extremist.

A more worrying possibility is the presence of nonstandard measurement error. Perhaps the cases where the party's candidates are not on the assumed side of the median voter—that is, cases where we have misclassified extremists versus moderates, potentially—also tend to be cases where, for other reasons, the party is expected to do better in the general election. Could this produce a bias in favor of moderate nominees? No. Even among these cases, we still compare the (roughly) half of cases where the moderate wins the primary to the other (roughly) half of cases where the extremist wins. Thus, issues like this will be differenced out.

Finally, it is possible that the candidates scaled as moderates are different from extremist candidates in other ways besides ideology. How do we know these other factors aren't driving the observed penalty? We don't! This is why it was important to lay out the precise research goals earlier in the chapter. The goal is not to isolate the causal effect of ideology itself. Instead, we want to consider the actual choices that voters face. When voters in the general election receive the option to elect a more moderate candidate, they seize it. Whether or not this result is driven by ideology itself, it tells us that moderates who stand for office in the general election tend to make it into office. Legislative polarization is thus unlikely to be driven by the electoral choices of general-election voters, directly.

Summary: The Value of Studying Electoral Selection

Despite the enormous amount of research devoted to it, and despite tremendous popular interest in it, political scientists have reached no consensus on the question of whether moderate candidates are advantaged in U.S. elections. In this chapter, I have tried to explain this lack of consensus, and I have proposed a methodological framework for studying how elections select candidates of varying ideology for political office. The framework offers two core takeaways.

First, to understand the link between elections and legislative polarization, we want to study what I have called *electoral selection*: the tendency for electorates to select more-moderate or more-extreme candidates for political office. The framework has made clear why this is distinct from studying the ideological preferences of individual voters, and from studying the effect of candidate positioning. Second, the key empirical challenge of studying electoral selection is the need to measure the ideological positions of both winning and losing candidates. Historically, this has not been possible, but recent advances in studying candidate ideology using campaign contributions have opened new doors. Although there are concerns about the particularities of various methods for scaling candidates based on contributions, there are good reasons to believe their validity, and we can compare analyses using various methods to make sure our conclusions are not the result of a specific flaw with any specific technique.

Having laid out this framework, I now apply it in chapter 3 to show that U.S. House elections exhibit a strong on-average preference for more-moderate candidates.

The Electoral Preference
for Moderates

The purpose of this chapter is to show that U.S. House of Representatives elections favor more ideologically moderate candidates, on average. Many people don't believe U.S. elections favor moderates because they see so much extremism in our legislatures and in our public discourse. This is a tempting fallacy. As is the case with so many questions in the social sciences, our intuitions can lead us astray. Extremism in our legislatures does not necessarily indicate that elections favor extremists. Though there is room for many causes, our legislatures seem to be extreme mainly because voters are constrained to choose from a polarized set of candidates.

I first present new observational evidence that shows a positive association between candidate moderation and electoral performance. These analyses use the same types of assumptions from previous literature, laid out in chapter 2, but they improve on previous analyses because they are able to include both incumbents and nonincumbents. To my knowledge, these are the largest-scale studies of candidate ideology and electoral success conducted to date, using information on 24,123 U.S. House candidate positions estimated from more than six million donors.

To supplement these analyses, I present quasi-experimental evidence that nominating more-extreme candidates in close primary elections causes parties to perform much worse in the general election, on average. Using this regression discontinuity design, explained in chapter 2, I am able to hold district preferences fixed under assumptions weaker than those deployed in previous research. With this technique, I document substantial penalties to extremist nominees. When a party barely nominates an extremist instead of a more-moderate candidate, its general-election vote share drops precipitously.

The conclusion of all these analyses is clear. Using a variety of measurement and estimation strategies, I estimate that the U.S. House electorate strongly prefers more-moderate candidates, on average. I conclude that the polarization of our legislatures is not primarily due to voters favoring more-extreme candidates.

New Observational Evidence That Voters Prefer Moderates

Taking advantage of the large data set of CFScores, I can extend and confirm the results of the previous literature that studies voters' choices over candidates.

I start with graphical evidence. Figure 3.1 shows that moderate candidates outperform more-extreme candidates systematically in House elections. Using the roughly twenty-four thousand candidate-election observations in the DIME data set, including all candidates in the primary and

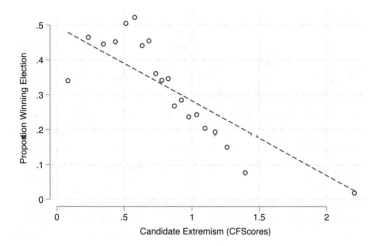

FIGURE 3.1. The electoral success of moderate candidates, U.S. House of Representatives, 1980–2014. This scatterplot shows the proportion of U.S. House candidates who win election across binned averages of the estimated ideological extremism of candidates, using CFscores, based on about 24,000 candidate-election observations in the DIME data set. *Note:* Points are averages in equal-sample-sized bins of the distance from the extremism variable, generated using the Stata binscatter package.

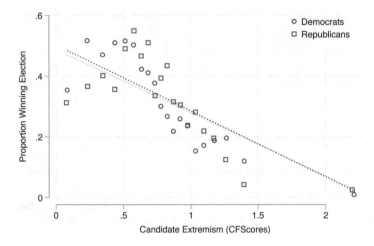

FIGURE 3.2. The electoral success of moderate candidates by party, U.S. House of Representatives, 1980–2014. As this scatterplot shows, using the same analysis as in figure 3.1 but split
by party, the association between ideological extremism and electoral success is the same
among both Democrats (circles) and Republicans (squares). *Note*: Points are averages in equal-
sample-sized bins of the distance from the extremism variable, generated using the Stata
binscatter package.

general elections, I first calculated the absolute value of each candidate's
CFscore, as a crude proxy for ideological extremism, following Canes-
Wrone, Brady, and Cogan (2002). I then computed binned averages which
reflect, within equal-sample-sized bins of the distance from the district's
ideology, the proportion of candidates who win election.

As the scatterplot in figure 3.1 shows, more-moderate candidates—that
is, candidates whose ideological positions are estimated to be farther from
zero—win election at a much higher rate. At larger and larger values of
this extremism variable, fewer and fewer candidates win election.

In figure 3.2, I performed the same analysis but splitting by party. The
phenomenon is consistent across both parties, as the overlapping scatterplots show. Among Republicans and Democrats, candidates whose estimated positions are closer to those of the average donor win elections at
a higher rate.

Could these patterns simply reflect differences between incumbents and
nonincumbents? We might suspect that incumbents look more moderate in
their campaign contributions because they receive more money from access-
oriented donors (Fouirnaies and Hall 2014). To evaluate this possibility

quickly, figure 3.3 presents the same kind of analysis, but only for open-seat races where no incumbent is present in either party. We continue to see the same relationship. (The overall percent of candidates who win elections is lower in open-seat races, as the reader may notice when looking at the vertical axis, because open-seat races tend to attract a large number of primary candidates, increasing the denominator of the outcome variable).

These simple scatterplots do not address a variety of issues that confound the association between candidate positions and electoral success. As the methodological discussion in the previous section made clear, the key issue is the possibility that more-extreme candidates run for office in districts that prefer more-extreme candidates, which could lead us to underestimate the advantage of moderate candidates. These graphs combine data across all districts, and so they potentially fall victim to this issue.

As a first step toward addressing this key issue of selection bias, in appendix 2 I replicate the regressions from the designs of Canes-Wrone, Brady, and Cogan (2002) and Ansolabehere, Snyder, and Stewart (2001), using contribution-based scalings that allow us to study both incumbents and nonincumbents. I provide technical details on the setup in appendix 2. Both designs show consistent evidence of a large association between candidate moderation and electoral success.

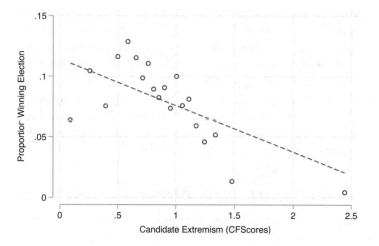

FIGURE 3.3. The electoral success of moderate candidates in open-seat races, U.S. House of Representatives, 1980–2014. This scatterplot shows that the pattern observed in figure 3.1 holds even when the candidates are not incumbents. *Note:* Points are averages in equal-sample-sized bins of the distance from the extremism variable, generated using the Stata binscatter package.

Could these results be driven by the use of CFScores? To make sure this is not the case, I next redo the analysis in appendix 2 using the DW-DIME scalings, which are set up to recover DW-NOMINATE scores. As a reminder, this technique addresses the fear that CFScores reflect partisanship rather than ideology, as I discussed in chapter 2. I again find similar results. I also reestimate the results using the Hall-Snyder scalings, which explicitly address the threat of strategic donating. Again, I find similar results.

To further bolster our confidence that the results are not driven by the particularities of these scalings, the formal results in appendix 2 also control directly for the total amount of money each candidate raises. The finding that more-moderate candidates outperform more-extreme candidates is true even making comparisons only among more-moderate and more-extreme candidates who raise similar amounts of money.

Quasi-Experimental Evidence That Voters Prefer Moderates

In this section, I lay out a quasi-experimental approach to studying the performance of candidates of varying ideological positions. Instead of using an observable proxy for district ideology, here I use the quasi-random outcomes of primary elections to approximate an experiment in which candidates of differing ideology are "randomly" assigned to stand for office in the general election. Because this is like an experiment, this means that districts that get candidates with varying ideologies will be otherwise alike, on average—including, crucially, in the underlying preferences of their constituents. This approach is thus another way to attempt to hold fixed the unobserved median voter. The results are highly consistent with those found in the previous section; when more-extreme candidates beat out more-moderate candidates to win the nomination, they do much worse in the general election.

An Example: Arkansas Second Congressional District, 2010

Before the 2010 elections, Rep. Vic Snyder (D-AR), the incumbent for the Second Congressional District, announced his retirement. The Second District contained Little Rock and had historically been represented by Democrats, but amid the rise of Tea Party candidates and the Republican backlash against Barack Obama's presidential victory in 2008, it was expected to be competitive in the general election.

A number of candidates entered the open-seat race in both parties. On the Democratic side, two front-runners emerged: Joyce Elliott, a veteran state legislator who was majority whip in the state senate at the time, and Robbie Wills, also a veteran state legislator and speaker in the Arkansas House of Representatives. When neither candidate secured a majority in the primary election, they entered a highly contentious runoff primary where they competed head-to-head for the Democratic nomination.

Elliott offered a platform of what might be called national Democratic policies. Most contentiously, she strongly supported increased gun control, even though she was running for an office in Arkansas, a state not known for its widespread support for gun control. Based on the mix of campaign contributions she received, Elliott's overall ideological positioning was roughly consistent with that of Speaker Nancy Pelosi.

Wills, on the other hand, was a prominent businessman who opposed gun control and, surprisingly for a member of the Democratic Party, the Affordable Care Act (nicknamed "Obamacare"). With a gimlet eye on the general election and the conservative tilt of the 2010 elections, Wills repeatedly labeled Elliott an "extremist," sending out a controversial mailer that declared Elliott "unelectable" due to her far-left views (Wickline 2010).

Comparing Elliott's and Wills's positions helps make clear the research strategy. For our purposes, Elliott is more extreme than Wills, not because we are making any judgment on whose views are extreme in any absolute sense, but purely based on their position *in relation to each other*. All facts—data based on campaign contributions, patterns of endorsements, newspaper accounts, and even the rhetoric of the candidates themselves—point to Elliott being farther to the left than Wills. As such, for this research purpose, we label her the more extreme candidate.

How did the election turn out? In a nod to the results that follow, Elliott, the "extremist," eked out a close victory over Wills in the runoff primary—and then went on to lose the general election by 14 percentage points.

Large Electoral Penalty to Extremists

Following my earlier work (Hall 2015), here I scale candidates using the contribution-based method (from Hall and Snyder 2015a). The advantage to this method is that it only uses money that candidates raise in primary elections *before they are incumbents*. This ensures that the scalings are not driven by the strategic donating of incumbent-seeking contributors, and it also ensures that the scalings are not "post-treatment" since they are

CHAPTER THREE

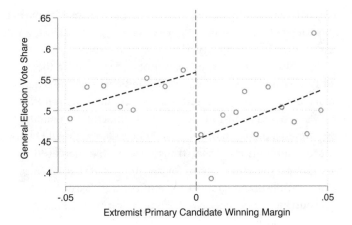

FIGURE 3.4. The penalty for nominating extremists, U.S. House of Representatives, 1980–2012. Using the Hall-Snyder Ideology Measure, this diagram shows that when extremists barely win competitive primaries (just to the right of the vertical line in the middle of the figure), their party does much worse in the general election than when they just barely lose and the more moderate candidate wins the nomination (just to the left of the vertical line). *Note*: Points are averages in equal-sample-sized bins of extremist win margin. Lines are from OLS estimated to the raw data (not the bins), estimated separately for each side of the discontinuity. Scatterplot generated using Stata binscatter command.

based only on donations from before the candidate wins office, if he or she wins office. For similar regression discontinuity (RD) estimates that show the robustness of the design using CFScores, dynamic CFScores, and DW-DIME scores, see Hall and Thompson forthcoming.

Data on U.S. House primary and general elections is compiled from primary sources by Ansolabehere et al. (2010) and updated by those authors to include subsequent years. I focus on elections in the years 1980–2012 to match the data on candidate positions. I keep all primary elections in which at least two candidates have donor scores. Among these elections, I analyze the two candidates with the top-two vote totals, and I calculate each candidate's share of the top-two vote total.[1]

Figure 3.4 shows the main result. The horizontal axis reflects the vote-share winning margin of the extremist candidate in the primary election. When this variable is negative, the more-moderate candidate wins nomination; when it is positive, the extremist does. The vertical axis reflects the vote share the winning primary candidate received in the general election. To make the empirical pattern clear, each point in the plot is the average vote share in equal-sample-sized bins of the extremist primary candidate winning margin.

The RD estimate is the instantaneous fall in the rate of winning that occurs when parties go from just barely nominating the moderate to just barely nominating the extremist. As we can see in the figure, this drop is sharp. With the moderate nominee "randomly" winning the primary, parties receive roughly 55 percent of the general-election vote, on average. But when the extremist instead "randomly" wins the nomination, the party receives roughly 45 percent—a 10 percentage-point penalty.

In appendix 2, I present more formal econometric results. These results are consistent with the graph. Regardless of what specification I use, or whether we look at vote share or victory, there is a tremendously large penalty to nominating more-extreme candidates. As I have hastened to stress, these estimates do not isolate the causal effect of candidate positions; instead, they indicate general-election voters' marked preference for the types of candidates who offer more-moderate positions.

Replicating the Results with State Legislators

It is always important to ensure that results are not driven by the particular scaling strategy used. In particular, as I have discussed in other parts of the book, we might be worried that candidates who are scaled as moderate based on their campaign contributions are not actually moderate at all. I have already given theoretical reasons why we should not be overly worried about this issue; because strategic campaign contributing is a small portion of all donations, we are unlikely to conflate moderate candidates with those predicted to do well, electorally. Nevertheless, empirical ways to address this issue are obviously valuable. Here, I replicate the RD estimates of the effect of extremist nominations without using campaign contributions. To do so, I focus on primary elections for the House that take place between two state legislators. For these cases, I can evaluate their ideology based on their roll-call votes in state legislatures, identifying moderates and extremists without looking at their campaign contributions.

Table A2.8 in appendix 2 presents the results. Using this completely different scaling strategy, we again find large penalties to nominating extremists.

Summary: Voters' Choices Do Not Drive Polarization

In this chapter, I have applied the methodological framework from chapter 2 to study how U.S. House elections favor candidates of different ideologies. Despite popular rhetoric to the contrary, House elections actually appear to favor more-moderate candidates, on average. This phenomenon helps explain the simulation results from chapter 1, which showed that the majority of legislative polarization is due to the set of people who run for office rather than the choices voters make among candidates.

The results suggest, but cannot prove, that voters would elect more moderates if more ran for office. Chapter 5 presents some preliminary evidence in favor of this claim.

CHAPTER FOUR

Polarization and the Devaluing of Office

A political system unable to kindle ambitions for office is as much in danger of breaking down as one unable to restrain ambitions.—Joseph A. Schlesinger, *Ambition and Politics*

Thirty hours is what they tell you you should spend [fundraising]. And it's discouraging good people from running for public office. I could give you names of people who've said, "You know, I'd like to go to Washington and help fix problems, but I don't want to go to Washington and become a mid-level telemarketer, dialing for dollars, for crying out loud."—Rick Nolan (D-MN), *60 Minutes*

Because most accounts of the rise of legislative polarization focus on voters, they rarely consider how the design of our political institutions encourages more-extreme people to run for office and discourages more-moderate people from running for office. In chapter 1, I laid out an argument for why the question "who wants to run?" is key for explaining the rise in polarization in the U.S. House or Representatives. My argument focuses on how the costs and benefits of running for office—factors determined by our American political institutions—create differential incentives for more-moderate versus more-extreme citizens. I claim that these costs and benefits have changed, over time, leading to more polarization in our legislatures.

In this chapter I examine this claim directly. These costs and benefits are, for the most part, impossible to observe and measure. As such, the discussions that follow will mix quantitative data with qualitative evidence, leaning heavily on scholarly accounts, journalistic reports, and quotes from candidates themselves.

I begin by discussing changes to the landscape of campaign finance, which have compelled candidates to raise more money from more donors over time. Because fundraising requires time-consuming effort and is widely considered unpleasant, these changes have made running for office less appealing.

Next, I discuss changes to the media environment, which have similarly made becoming a candidate less appealing. Most individuals value their privacy, and whereas media coverage of politics is a vital component of our democracy, there is no denying that modern media coverage involves personality-driven aspects that are unpleasant for those under scrutiny.

I then turn to changes in the benefits of holding office, starting with legislator pay. Because pay raises are so politically explosive—and because members of Congress are forced to set their own pay—salary for members of Congress has not kept up with inflation. Indeed, salaries are now approaching lows not seen since the previous era of high polarization around the turn of the twentieth century.

Next, I explore how the job of legislator has changed, with declining opportunities to influence the policymaking process. The increasing tendency for the majority party to centralize agenda power has decreased the appeal of being an individual legislator. We see evidence of this change in how leadership makes committee assignments, in the decline of staffers allocated to committees, and in the increase of leadership-driven, bicameral "ping-pong" legislation, as opposed to the more traditional use of conference committees.

Finally, I offer a more speculative discussion that places these changes in historical context. I connect the current devaluing of politics to the early twentieth century, the previous era of high polarization in Congress. The early twentieth century was another time when parties gained power in the legislature and individual legislators lost influence. This observation suggests the possibility of a feedback loop in which initial increases in polarization tend to alter the organization of the legislature, dissuading more-moderate citizens from running for office and further increasing polarization. Though I do not take much away from over-time correlations, it is worth mentioning that this previous era of high polarization was also an era of unusually low legislative salaries.

All in all, looking at both the costs of running for office and the benefits of holding office, we see that the incentives for individuals to run for Congress have declined. This matters for polarization because, as I explained in chapter 1, this devaluing of office disproportionately deters more-moderate individuals from seeking office.

The Growing Burden of Fundraising

The demands of campaign finance, a key driver of the costs of running for office, have risen sharply since the late twentieth century. I start with some simple facts. Figure 4.1 shows average total campaign receipts and disbursements across all U.S. House races by year, in inflation-adjusted 2014 U.S. dollars, as collated in the Database on Ideology, Money in Politics, Elections (DIME) data set. Since 1980, and especially since 1990, candidates have raised and spent more money. The average amount raised and spent has more than doubled since 1980.

These changes are only on average. Figure 4.2 compares the full distribution of campaign spending for 1980 and 2014, in the left and right panels, respectively. As the histograms show, this over-time change is not the result of a few outlier candidates—instead there has been a pronounced rightward shift in campaign spending, measured in inflation-adjusted U.S. dollars, in House races.

In isolation, the fact that more money is raised might not mean fundraising is more difficult; perhaps candidates are simply able to get larger

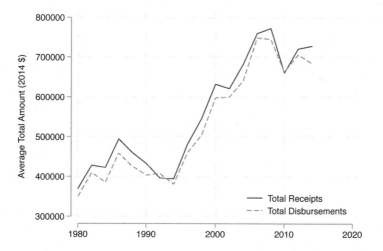

FIGURE 4.1. Increases in total campaign money raised and spent, U.S. House of Representatives, 1980–2014. As this graph shows, candidates for the U.S. House are forced to raise more money, and spend more money, than ever before. *Note*: Amounts are shown in inflation-adjusted 2014 U.S. dollars, as collated in the DIME data set.

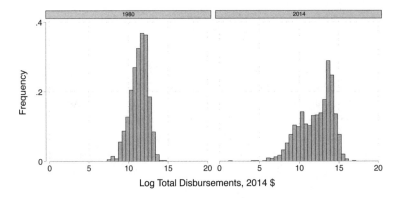

FIGURE 4.2. Distribution of candidate expenditures, U.S. House of Representatives, 1980 and 2014. As these two histograms comparing the full distribution of campaign spending for 1980 and 2014 show, there has been a pronounced rightward shift in campaign spending. *Note*: Amounts are measured in inflation-adjusted U.S. dollars.

amounts of money from the same donors as before. This is probably unlikely, since individuals and political action committees (PACs) are limited in how much they can contribute, but we can investigate it directly in the data. Figure 4.3 plots the average number of donors from whom candidates raise money (also from the DIME data set). Candidates are seeking donations from more and more donors over time. In 2010, candidates received donations from almost exactly four times as many donors as in 1990, on average. This number has already doubled again since 2010 (even despite a small dip in 2012).

Research on campaign fundraising accords with these over-time patterns. According to Magleby and Nelson (2010, 3), "The consequences of the money chase are also serious for Congress as an institution. Because limits on what individuals and PACs can give do not take account of inflation, members must constantly expand their donor base. *This takes more and more time and effort.*" The authors summarize, "*in short, fundraising has become a larger part of the job description of House and Senate members . . .*" (4; emphasis mine).

Politicians themselves have also noticed these changes. In remarks in the *Congressional Record* in 1998, already on the steep upward curve of the growth in spending as shown in figure 4.3, Lee Hamilton (D-IN) declared, "Candidates today are engaged in an *ever-escalating effort to raise money*. In 1976, my campaign cost about $100,000; in the last election, it cost $1 million. The practical effect of the money chase is that *candidates*

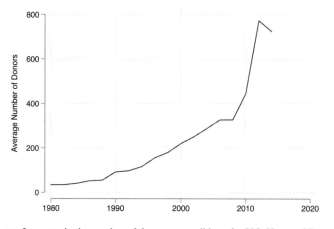

FIGURE 4.3. Increases in the number of donors to candidates for U.S. House of Representatives, 1980–2014. The graph shows that the average number of donors from whom candidates raise money has increased markedly since the beginning of the twenty-first century. *Note*: Numbers of donors as collated in the DIME data set.

spend more time raising money and less time meeting with constituents and doing their legislative work."[1] After announcing his retirement, Tom Harkin, former Senator and member of Congress, told the *Washington Post* that being a legislator is "not as much fun" as it used to be, because people are "out raising money" instead of meeting with fellow members and building camaraderie (O'Keefe 2013).

This fundraising is costly for candidates because it is difficult, time-consuming, and unpleasant. Speaking at a 2009 congressional hearing about a bill to implement a program for federal funding of congressional campaigns, Rep. Dan Lungren (R-CA) captured the feelings of many congressional candidates:

> I am going to put it on the record: *I hate raising money for campaigns*. The only two people I know who enjoyed it both went to prison. And I won't use their names. But I hate it. It is the least attractive part of this job. I can sell ideas, I can ask for support for others. I have a great deal of difficulty—and my campaign finance people are listening, and they would probably say don't say it—but I have a great deal of difficulty making the close on asking for money. It is the most difficult.
>
> And now we have in our campaign coverage by the reporters, they start to judge whether you are a good candidate, whether you have got good prospects

depending on how much money you have got in your account. Read the stories now. They are about how much money did you have this quarter. So the very press that is telling us maybe this is what we ought to do is the very press that is making this part of the horse race, and that is a terrible tragedy.[2]

Speaking at the same hearing, Rep. John Larson (D-CT) echoed these thoughts: "All of my colleagues are principled people who would rather be doing just about anything else, as you bore witness to, than making fundraising calls, attending fundraising breakfasts, lunches, dinners, you name it." Fundraising, these members of Congress say, is an unpleasant but necessary activity—one that is costly to perform but required to win and hold office.

The need to fundraise has grown much more acute since 1980, to the point that members of Congress are now told to spend most of the day "dialing for dollars." David Jolly (R-FL) gave a particularly jarring description of this state of affairs to *60 Minutes*: "It is a cult-like boiler room on Capitol Hill where sitting members of Congress, frankly I believe, are compromising the dignity of the office they hold by sitting in these sweatshop phone booths calling people asking them for money. And their only goal is to get $500 or $1,000 or $2,000 out of the person on the other end of the line. It's shameful. It's beneath the dignity of the office that our voters in our communities entrust us to serve" (O'Donnell 2016).

There are probably many reasons fundraising needs have grown so rapidly. The changing media landscape necessitates more and more ad buys at higher prices to communicate to voters. Technical innovations, both in terms of studying what types of strategies attract voters and in targeting specific voters with ads, have probably raised the returns to campaign spending, creating more upward pressure on fundraising. It is certainly possible that technology has also made it easier to raise money, but these gains seem to be outweighed by the increased demands. If fundraising is a "race to the bottom," in which each candidate must outwork the other to raise more money (as discussed in the next section), then any gains from technology will be immediately undone by increases in effort.

These needs have probably risen even more sharply since the U.S. Supreme Court's 2010 *Citizens United* decision, which lifted previous restrictions on campaign contributions from corporations. In the same *60 Minutes* interview cited earlier, Reid Ribble (R-WI) explained that "some of this is the result of *Citizens United*, the Supreme Court decision that opened up really [*sic*] corporate dollars into the system. And so, if you want to have your own voice, if you want your voice to be heard as opposed to some out-side group speaking for you, you better—you better do your job and raise enough money that you can" (O'Donnell 2016).

Costs like these deter moderate people from running for office. Can-didates themselves believe this claim. Jolly, himself a relatively moderate Republican, told 60 Minutes, "At the end of the day, if you tell me that the only way to be a United States senator is to raise $100 million in Florida, then I'm not the next United States senator from the state of Florida. And that's OK. It's a shame for the system, but it's fine for me" (O'Donnell 2016). Hamilton expressed a similar view: "Too many talented and ener-getic people simply choose not to run because they don't have the stomach to get into the money chase" (O'Donnell 2016).

The Race to the Bottom

The way in which I have described campaign finance is drastically dif-ferent from how most reformers talk about it. For reformers, the focus is largely on the corrupting influence of money in politics. I do not deny that money may corrupt. But *even if* money had no corrupting influence, it creates a "race to the bottom" that leaves candidates and voters worse off.

The situation is much like that with steroids in professional baseball. Suppose (as is almost certainly true) that steroids are bad for your health but make you a better baseball player. Like elections, performance in base-ball is relative; your success depends not just on some absolute benchmark of quality but on doing better than your opponents. Realizing the need to outperform, any individual player might think about doing steroids to get an edge but might prefer not to do them *if he knew that no one else was going to do them, either.* There's the rub. So long as a completely credible detection and punishment system does not exist, players will feel compelled to do steroids because of their belief that other players are doing them, too.

The dynamic in politics is the same. Any given candidate might prefer to spend less time fundraising. But each candidate sees that other candi-dates are fundraising more, and more, and more, forcing their opponents to respond in kind. People cannot cut back their efforts so long as they be-lieve that their opponents won't do likewise. Foreseeing this vicious cycle, moderate would-be candidates may choose not to run in the first place.

A potential solution to this race to the bottom is the same as in base-ball: a powerful reform that credibly promises all candidates that no one can outraise the other beyond a certain point. Like rigorous steroid testing, campaign finance reform can reassure candidates that they don't need to spend four hours a day fundraising because neither they nor their opponents are allowed to. Implementing such an idea is extremely difficult, though. Even putting aside issues of constitutional law for the moment, limiting fundraising in the right way is tricky. To see this, we can look to the laboratory of the U.S. states. The states employ a dazzling variety of campaign finance laws. The two most directly relevant for our purposes are the public funding of elections and low limits on the size of campaign contributions.

Public Funding of Elections

In an earlier work (Hall 2014), I studied the effects of public-funding programs in the U.S. states. Three states have passed these programs relatively recently—Arizona, Connecticut, and Maine—and two more, Minnesota and Wisconsin, passed them in the 1970s. Though the precise details vary in important ways across states, the basic idea in all five is that candidates can apply for and, after they meet some minimal fundraising requirements, receive public funding in lieu of private fundraising. Ideally, public funding removes significant fundraising burdens from candidates, making the electoral process easier and encouraging more people to run for office.

The effects of public funding, however, have not been as expected. Although, as I showed (Hall 2014), electoral competition has increased in states that implemented public-funding programs, the programs have also markedly *increased* legislative polarization. Why?

To qualify for public funding, candidates must first raise small (usually five-dollar) donations from a fixed number of individual donors. This seemingly small barrier alters the donor landscape in important ways. Without public funding, candidates raise significant amounts of money from interest groups. With public funding, these groups no longer participate in campaign finance in the same way (although they can still donate to candidates who opt out of public funding). The result is that elections become much more dominated by individual donors, and we know from a large body of scholarship that individual donors support more ideologically extreme candidates than do interest-group donors (see, e.g., Bonica 2014).

The nuanced effects of public-funding programs point to the deeper difficulties of encouraging more-moderate candidates through campaign

finance reform. Put simply, most reforms have many unintended consequences. It is difficult to create a reform that isolates only a single factor—
such as the difficulty of running for office. Another, similar reform exhibits
this same issue well. Just as some states have experimented with public
funding, many others have experimented with limiting the size of individual and interest-group contributions, respectively. Barber (2015) studies
the effects of these limits, and the results point to the same underlying
phenomenon. In places where individuals can donate more, legislators are
more extreme; in places where groups can contribute more, legislators are
more moderate.

Low Limits on Campaign Contributions

Barber's results do suggest that limiting individual contributions strictly
may reduce polarization (Barber 2015). However, it is impossible to know
whether this has anything to do with changing the costs of running for office or if it simply reflects that, when individuals can't contribute much, the
types of candidates who benefit from individual contributions suffer. In
addition, before recommending such a tack, we might worry about other
effects it could have. Leaving only interest groups to contribute, for example, would certainly raise suspicions of corruption. Campaign finance
also likely enhances voter engagement and voter information (through
candidate advertising, etc.), so the losses may far exceed the gain of more
moderate representation. These are trade-offs that would be difficult to
resolve even if we had any certainty of the effects of such reforms on all the
various outcomes we care about.

   The reform that might more directly solve the race-to-the-bottom problem is a limit on campaign spending itself, rather than on contributions.
If candidates are only allowed to spend a certain amount, then there is no
reason for them to raise more than that amount. Although this would be
the most logical solution, it is a no-go in the United States, where such limits are unconstitutional for the time being.

   Fouirnaies (2016) studies the effects of such limits by taking advantage
of historical changes to spending limits in constituencies in the United
Kingdom. These changes, Fouirnaies shows, noticeably changed campaigns and election outcomes. When constituencies quasi-randomly had
higher limits on candidate spending, incumbents did better and elections
became more partisan. Although Fouirnaies has no direct measure of ideology, fewer elections are contested by multiple parties when spending

limits rise. This finding suggests, as I have argued, that higher spending limits make campaigning more difficult and deter many would-be candidates, particularly moderate ones.

Increasing Media Scrutiny of Candidates

Fundraising is not the only cost of running for office. As Lungren's earlier quotation alluded to, media coverage of congressional campaigns seems to have changed, in its content and its tenor, over the same period that polarization has been growing in U.S. legislatures.

Bai (2014) offers a striking account of this change through the lens of a single event: the Gary Hart scandal of 1987. The book's subtitle—*The Week Politics Went Tabloid*—summarizes its argument. Exploring Gary Hart's media-fueled fall from grace, Bai argues that the media have changed the way they cover political actors in the United States, focusing more and more on personal details that may or may not be relevant for evaluating the quality of candidates. Gary Hart's alleged affair with Donna Rice, which precipitated the end of his presidential campaign, was, according to Bai (2014, 24), among the first personal, "tabloid" scandals of American political officials—the first of many: "Hart's humiliation had been the first in a seemingly endless parade of exaggerated scandals and public floggings, the harbinger of an age when the threat of instant destruction would mute any thoughtful debate, and when even the perception of some personal imperfection could obliterate, or at least eclipse, whatever else had accumulated in the public record."

Hart himself, in his speech announcing the end of his campaign, worried about the changing role of the media in politics, stating, "We're all going to have to seriously question the system for selecting our national leaders, that reduces the press of this nation to hunters and presidential candidates to being hunted, that has reporters in bushes, false and inaccurate stories printed, photographers peeking in our windows, swarms of helicopters hovering over our roof, and my very strong wife close to tears because she can't even get in her own house at night without being harassed" (*Los Angeles Times* 1987). Though speaking about running for president, his sentiments extend readily to the coverage that candidates for other offices, such as the U.S. House, receive in smaller doses but with similar tenor.

Potential candidates themselves appear to be keenly aware of the toll the media can take on those who enter the poitical arena. Lawless and

Fox (2005, 126), interviewing potential candidates, quote a California attorney who contends, "The intrusion into one's privacy that comes with
a campaign is such that one would have to be insane to run for office."
Sabato (1993, 210–11) makes an early and clear version of this argument:
"The second troubling consequence of modern media coverage for the
political system has to do with the recruitment of candidates and public
servants. Simply put, the price of power has been raised dramatically, far
too high for many outstanding potential officeholders. . . . American society today is losing the services of many exceptionally talented individuals
who would make outstanding contributions to the commonwealth, but
who understandably will not subject themselves and their loved ones to
abusive, intrusive press coverage" (Sabato 1993, 210–11). Sutter (2006)
formalizes this logic, showing how "privacy costs" of running for office can
affect the set of people willing to become candidates. As Sutter (2006, 38)
concludes, "The proliferation of frenzies and expansion of the range of
personal issues subject to scrutiny raises the expected cost to good people
of running for public office." Though Sutter's work focuses on a broader
concept of candidate "quality" and not ideology, the argument can readily
extend to the idea of moderate versus less-moderate candidates, as in the
theoretical discussion from chapter 3 of this book.

It is difficult to offer hard, quantitative evidence for the claim that the
media are making running for office harder. But at the very least, experience suggests that the claim is true. The twenty-four-hour news cycle,
manufactured scandals to fill airtime, and the expansion of social media
have all lent a circus atmosphere to our elections. Astonishing amounts of
time are devoted to absolutely inane details of candidates' lives. This apparent hunger to convert political coverage into entertainment does not
come without costs. Whether or not such coverage expands the knowledge of citizens who would not otherwise engage in politics (Baum 2002;
Prior 2003), it surely makes people think twice before running for office.
Although changing the way the media cover politics seems difficult, and
maybe impossible, we should acknowledge the likelihood that it is preventing good people from becoming candidates for our legislatures.

Declining Pay for U.S. House Members

So far in this chapter, I have discussed salient drivers of the costs of running for
office. I now turn to the benefits of holding office, for those who run and win.

Holding office conveys many benefits. Officeholders have the chance to influence policy, to bring issues to the attention of government and voters, and to enjoy a degree of prestige. Separate from these various opportunities, legislators also receive monetary compensation for their efforts. Though pay is far from the only benefit of office—and would-be candidates are likely to seek office for myriad reasons—it is an obvious first variable to examine in considering how the benefits of holding office have changed over time. In this section, I show that House salaries have declined steeply, in real terms, since the mid-twentieth century.

To examine how U.S. House members are paid, I collected data on the salaries of members of Congress from the Congressional Research Service. Though there are a few positions within the House that get paid more (e.g., Speaker), the vast majority of members receive the same, fixed salary. To see how legislator pay has changed over time, I use data from the U.S. Bureau of Labor Statistics Consumer Price Index (CPI) to correct for inflation, reporting all salaries in terms of 2014 U.S. dollars.

Figure 4.4 graphs U.S. House member salaries over time. As the gray solid line shows, legislator salaries have declined noticeably in real terms since the 1970s. In 1969, at the historic peak of legislative pay, members of the U.S. House were paid $42,500—or about $274,000 in 2014 dollars. Today, members are paid $174,000. Though this amount is nominally higher than that in 1969, it constitutes a decrease of just over one-third (35 percent) in real terms due to inflation. This is a large decrease.[3]

Simply looking at the change in how much members of the House get paid misses deeper costs in holding elected office. The dashed line in figure 4.4 attempts to hint at these opportunity costs by showing the difference between House salaries and the average U.S. income over time. As we see, this gap has shrunk noticeably since 1969, too. In fact, when we consider the difference from the average income, we see that pay for members of the House has fallen to levels not seen since the early twentieth century.

Correlation between Lower Pay and Polarization

Chapter 5 will explore some causal links among legislator salary, who runs for office, and polarization. Interestingly, figure 4.4 suggests such a link. The decline in salaries since 1969 has put current salaries close to previous lows in the early twentieth century—and, when compared to average U.S. incomes, the decline has already reached these lows. As figure 1.1 in chapter 1 showed, the early twentieth century was the previous

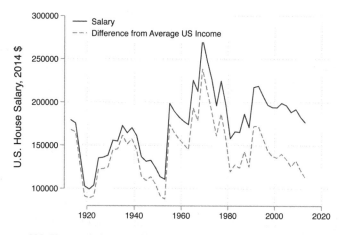

FIGURE 4.4. U.S. House salaries over time, adjusted for inflation. As this graph shows, after peaking in 1969, salaries for members of Congress have declined 35 percent in real terms. The gap between legislators' salaries and the average U.S. income also has narrowed, indicating a greater opportunity cost for holding office. *Note*: Salary data from Congressional Research Service. Amounts are shown in inflation-adjusted 2014 U.S. dollars.

high-polarization era in American politics. Correlating two time series is not a way to establish a causal relationship, but the analyses in chapter 5 will offer evidence for exactly such a relationship; legislative polarization appears to be higher when pay for legislators is lower.

Lower Pay Affecting Who Runs

Whatever the reason, legislator salaries are significantly lower today than they were in the 1960s and 1970s. This drop constitutes a meaningful decrease in the benefits of holding office. Although there are many other benefits of holding office—some of which I will discuss shortly—salaries in office are an important and necessary component of how we compensate citizens for holding office. When legislator salaries are higher, all else equal, then more people, and different types of people, will be willing to run.

Scholarly discussions with potential candidates support this view. Though focused primarily on the gender gap in seeking political office, Lawless and Fox (2005) present a bevy of data on the calculations of potential candidates, who are "forced to deal with the financial tradeoffs involved in holding elective office" (133). The authors detail a conversation with a Kentucky attorney who has considered running for office but concludes, "My job allows me a lot of comfort. If I ran, I'd have to take off a great deal of time and that would put too big a dent in my pocket" (133). Salary is clearly one of the important inputs into whether would-be candidates run for office or stay out and maintain their current jobs.

One probable result of the lessened salaries for legislators is that, by and large, only wealthy people will run for office (the fact that wealthy people can fund their own campaigns is a separate factor that also encourages them to run). An article entitled "Why Is Congress a Millionaires Club?" (Condon 2012), for example, documents the high wealth of members of Congress compared to the public. The article reads: "As a congressional candidate, 'every waking minute of every day is devoted to that campaign,' said Doug Heye, a former spokesman for the Republican National Committee. 'It requires an extraordinary amount of time, and it becomes difficult for a lot of people if you have a full-time job . . . When you've got a mortgage to pay and college tuition and braces to pay for, those kinds of day-to-day, real-life expenses come before putting six months into a campaign.' "

It is likely that ultrawealthy people are running for office precisely because they enjoy doing so—their wealth permits them to undertake activities for what might be called recreational purposes. People who enjoy holding office are likely to be those with stronger and more ideological views. Were salaries higher—a counterfactual scenario I consider in chapter 5—then people who view politics as an important and valuable job, rather than as an idle activity of the rich and ideological, might become more willing to run.

The decreasing salaries of legislators also mean that the *opportunity costs* of running for office are higher than ever. Fiorina (1994) made a novel argument about opportunity costs and the decision to serve in the legislature. Focusing on state legislatures, he argues that the professionalization of legislatures advantaged Democrats because Republican candidates tended to be drawn from higher-paying occupations. When the legislature becomes more professionalized, these higher-earning individuals can less afford to make legislating a full-time job since they have to give up their lucrative jobs to do so.

The present argument is similar in spirit. When salaries in other, nonpolitical fields are higher, high-skilled people will face increased costs of entering politics because they must forgo these other career opportunities. Those willing to run for office, regardless of whether they are of higher or lower "quality," will be those more willing to forgo these other opportunities—likely people who hold more-extreme ideological views and value the chance to hold office, or fear more what will happen if they don't hold office, or both.

What About the Revolving Door?

In examining compensation, I have focused only on the salaries members of Congress receive, but a major value of holding office might be the chance to make money after leaving. In the so-called revolving door, members of Congress sometimes go on to be lobbyists or consultants or to otherwise parlay their political experience into private-sector remuneration. Is this a major value of holding office, and is it high enough to offset the fall in direct compensation?

Answering this question is difficult. Establishing that former House members become lobbyists is insufficient to conclude that there are substantial monetary benefits to holding office, because we need to know the counterfactual outcome: how much money would these individuals have gone on to earn if, instead of winning a seat in the House, they had worked at some other job instead? For the set of people who are able to win office, these opportunity costs—that is, the other jobs they could have held—are likely to be high because members of the House are already unusually wealthy, relative to the general population, and are likely to come from high-earning occupations.

When we look at the average compensation of lobbyists, it is not at all obvious that former House members are earning more from lobbying than they could have if they had not become members of Congress. According to a report of the Sunlight Foundation, former members of Congress earned a median salary of roughly $260,000 as lobbyists in 2012 (Drutman and Furnas 2014). Although this number is greater than a congressional salary, it is smaller than the median salary earned by lobbyists coming from other, nonelected staff positions, which was roughly $300,000 in 2012. Furthermore, although $260,000 is an incredibly high salary relative to the median American—according to the U.S. Census Bureau (2017), the median household income was roughly $60,000 in 2016, for example—it would not be high for anyone taking a pay cut to run for Congress, who would by definition be making more than $174,000 before running for office. When we account for the fact that many members stay in Congress for many years before becoming lobbyists, if we try to extrapolate what they would have earned in the private sector had they not run for office, it seems plausible that they could earn just as much, if not more, by not running for office.

That being said, the numbers in the Sunlight Foundation report are crude; they reflect only the median earnings of registered lobbyists. Members of Congress might have many other ways of accumulating wealth after serving in office. In addition, the comparisons between lobbyists who were and were not members of Congress do not reflect the causal effect of serving in Congress.

Three studies try to address these issues empirically. Studying British politics, Eggers and Hainmueller (2009) use a regression discontinuity design comparing people who barely make it into office to those who barely do not make it into office to show that members of Parliament accrue significant extra wealth through holding office. Querubín and Snyder (2013) study nineteenth-century members of the U.S. Congress and find no returns to holding office, except during the Civil War, when opportunities for profiteering were rampant. As such, the results of these first two studies are decidedly mixed, though neither study examines modern-day House elections.

Most relevantly for our purposes, Palmer and Schneer (2016) show that modern-day U.S. senators become more likely than comparable nonlegislators to hold corporate board memberships, which pay generous salaries. This finding suggests the potential for senators to earn considerable money after serving in office, but since it is not possible to measure the total wealth of senators and nonsenators, we cannot know for sure how they compare. Though senators may serve on more corporate boards than nonsenators do, it is possible that nonsenators go on to earn more money in other ways. Perhaps more important, we have good reasons to think that these effects would be smaller for members of the House, an office of less importance than the Senate. Indeed, in follow-up work, Palmer and Schneer (2018) show that members of the House go on to serve on corporate boards at lower rates than those for members of the Senate.

There is no doubt that the revolving door is an important issue in American politics today, and an important source of value for former members of Congress. But it is not at all clear that it conveys nearly enough value to induce people to run for office, particularly people already in high-paying occupations.

Diminishing Chances to Influence Policy in the House

A substantial potential benefit of holding office is the chance to influence policy. An additional, more general benefit is to feel personally efficacious in one's career. In this section, I describe some of the reasons why these potential benefits have declined, over time—particularly, though not exclusively, for more-moderate would-be candidates. I will rely largely on the argument from Thomsen (2017), who offers a masterful account of how the ideological and partisan polarization of the House has diminished the value of being a moderate member of Congress.

The Centralizing of Party Agenda Power

Historically, members of the U.S. House wielded control over policy in large part by serving on committees relevant to their districts (Gilligan and Krehbiel 1987; Krehbiel 1990; Londregan and Snyder 1994; Shepsle 1978). From about 1945 up to the early 1970s, House committees were thought to possess considerable power, allowing committee members to push specific policies in their preferred directions and to block policy changes in their committee's jurisdiction that they did not like. The most powerful were the committee chairs, highly coveted positions assigned purely on the basis of seniority. The seniority system offered a simple career ladder to members of Congress; the longer they stayed in office, the more power they would accrue, and the more chances they would have to influence policy (among other privileges). For a moderate potential candidate, this system would seemingly be quite appealing; the moderate's heightened ability to gain repeated reelection, as I documented in chapter 3, would make the candidate likely, if he or she so desired, to ascend to a position of considerable power.

Starting in the early 1970s, though, majority-party Democrats pushed through a series of reforms stripping the committee system of power and strengthening the office of the Speaker of the House. In one of the most detailed accounts of the reforms, Rohde (1991) describes the numerous ways the Democratic Party went about strengthening the party leadership. The Democratic caucus removed the absolute right of the Speaker to choose committee chairs, subjecting assignments to an up-or-down vote and eroding the seniority system as a result. Within the same period, the caucus gave the Speaker new powers; the power to refer bills to multiple committees, for example, further shifted power from committees to party leadership, preventing as it did a single committee from obstructing the Speaker's agenda. These changes, Rohde argues, ensured that the Democratic Party—and not a set of senior committee chairs—would determine legislative policy.

In a previous journal article coauthored with my colleague Kenneth

Shepsle (Hall and Shepsle 2014), I argue that strengthening the leadership must come at a cost. The agenda power that the Democrats—and later, in the early 1990s, the majority-party Republicans—gave to their leadership came from senior (often Southern) committee chairs. The Democratic reforms of the 1970s sounded the death knell for powerful committees, signaling, as Rohde (1991) and others have argued, the end of committee government and the beginning of government by party leadership.

The Decline in Moderates' Influence

This dramatic change in how members of Congress legislate would not go unnoticed by potential candidates. While in the past the powerful committee system assured potential moderate candidates of a chance to possess influence, the party-led legislature offers no such thing. With a powerful majority-party leader, members are more like "foot soldiers" than individual crafters of policy. The bulk of legislation—including all significant bills—no longer runs the route from committee to conference committee to passage. Instead, party leaders coordinate on amendments, ping-ponging bills between the chambers and striking bargains at the party level. Though there is no doubt room for individual influence, it is far less than in the previous era of strong committees.

This decline hits moderates particularly hard. Thomsen (2014, 789) asserts that, because "party leaders who set the legislative agenda are now ideologues themselves . . . it would be difficult for moderates to advance their desired policies or obtain a leadership position in Congress." Thomsen (2017) shows that the candidate pool has polarized in part because serving in the modern U.S. House is increasingly a poor fit for ideological moderates. The author contends that "the value of congressional office has diminished as [moderates] have become more at odds with the rest of their party delegation. It is increasingly difficult for moderates to achieve their policy goals and advance within the party or chamber, and they have fewer like-minded colleagues to work and interact with in office" (Thomsen 2017, 6).

In support of this claim, Thomsen (2017) shows both that ideologically moderate state legislators do not run for the House as often as more extreme state legislators do—an analysis I will build on in chapter 5—and that more-moderate members of the House have retired at higher rates than more-extreme members in recent times. It seems clear that the benefits of office have declined, particularly for moderate candidates.

Partisanship and Disproportionate Costs

This discussion of the organization of the legislature and the benefits of office have gone beyond the theoretical model from chapter 1 in two important ways.

First, this discussion has focused on dynamics within the legislature that are not considered in the theoretical model I offered, which treated the entire legislature as a black box, with only each individual candidate's ideological positioning consequential for the candidate's election and subsequent behavior in office. Clearly, dynamics inside the legislature will affect each individual legislator's ability to influence the policy process. These dynamics include the partisan organization of the policy process (Aldrich and Rohde 2001; Cox and McCubbins 2005; F. Lee 2009) as well as the need to bargain across chambers and branches of government (Krehbiel 1998). Examination of these dynamics raises the question of why, in the theoretical model I proposed, voters consider only an individual candidate's ideological position and not the candidate's total influence into this complicated process. As I discussed in chapter 1, it is important to keep the theory tractable. The theory can be thought of as making the simple assumption that voters value position taking (Mayhew 1974), separate from the question of how influential their individual member of Congress will be in the complex dance that eventually produces policy.

Second, this chapter's discussion has considered the possibility that the benefits of holding office vary across the ideological spectrum, with benefits lower for more-moderate candidates and higher for more-extreme candidates. Though this is not shown in the basic model, it is in keeping with the extension sketched in appendix 1. Not surprisingly, if the benefits of office are higher for more-extreme candidates, we should expect to see even more ideological divergence in the set of people who run for office.

The Devaluing of Office in Historical Context

The focus of this book, as I discussed in chapter 1, is on the recent rise in polarization. Nevertheless, it is valuable to consider the broader historical context in which the recent devaluing of office is taking place. Though it is hard to measure, the costs and benefits of running for the House have waxed and waned over time. Sometimes, when legislative politics is organized around a single dimension of ideology, as it is today for the most part, the theory I have offered predicts a causal relationship between these costs and benefits and polarization. In other eras, these costs and benefits should deter certain types of people from running for office, but the way they vary from those who do run may not be ideological in nature.

The early twentieth century, which exhibited the previous all-time highs of ideological polarization in the House (see figure 1.1 in chapter 1) is one era that potentially fits well with the theory. Like the period from 1980 to today, in this earlier era the majority party noticeably centralized legislative authority in the House. Starting with Speaker Reed's famous defeat of dilatory tactics in 1890, the position of Speaker became increasingly powerful in the House (Cox and McCubbins 2005; Jenkins and Stewart 2012). Describing the Speaker's enormous power in this system, Hasbrouck (1927, 2) observed that the "strength lay in the Speaker's control over the fountain-heads of legislation: his power to appoint his friends to committees, the right of the Committee on Rules . . . to change the rules without notice, the Speaker's power of 'non-recognition,' and the use of the previous question and other devices to prevent amendments." The centralization of power did not go unnoticed. The Democratic Party platform in 1908 declared that Congress "has ceased to be a deliberative and executive body, but has come under the absolute domination of the Speaker, who has entire control of its deliberations and powers of legislation" (as quoted in Hasbrouck 1927, 3). Although many of the changes to House rules in that period have endured to present day (Cox and McCubbins 2005; Jenkins and Stewart 2012), the power of the majority party waned as polarization decreased into the mid-twentieth century, starting gradually with the revolt against Speaker Cannon in 1910 (Hasbrouck 1927).

Unfortunately, it is impossible to measure the ideological positions of the set of people who ran for the House at this time, because we lack data on campaign contributions or any other indicator of ideology available for both winning and losing candidates. Nevertheless, it is interesting to note that this era of high polarization was also an era of low legislative salaries. It is plausible that the devaluing of office during the early twentieth century—both due to the organization of the legislature, which weakened individual legislator's influence, and due to the low compensation of members of Congress—contributed to the high degree of polarization.

The dynamic in which polarization leads the majority party to centralize power in the legislature (explored theoretically in Aldrich and Rohde

2001; Aldrich, Rohde, and Tofias 2007; and Patty 2008, among others) also suggests an interesting feedback loop. If a legislature becomes more polarized, perhaps due to an initial wave of electoral success of more-extreme candidates, it may then centralize power in the legislature. This centralization, in turn, may dissuade future moderates from running for office, further increasing polarization.

Going further, this increase in polarization, if it leads to gridlock, may upset voters, who may become less willing to support compensating legislators highly. This fall in the benefits of office will further dissuade moderates from running and, in turn, further polarize the legislature. This vicious cycle raises the possibility of a "polarization trap" in which the existence of polarization encourages conditions that prevent polarization from decreasing.

Summary: The Devaluing of Political Office in the Modern Era

In chapter 1, I offered evidence that the rising polarization in the U.S. House is, in large part, the result of the polarization of the set of people who run for office. I used this evidence to motivate a theory in which fewer moderate people run for office when the costs of running are high or the benefits of holding office are low (or both). The point of this chapter has been to connect this theory to what has happened in the U.S. House in recent history. Changes to the campaign finance environment, to the nature of media coverage, to the pay of members of Congress, and to the organization of the internal workings of the House since 1980 have all conspired to devalue office.

Having argued that the conditions of the theory are met—that is, that rising costs and falling benefits are indeed a reality in the House—the next question to ask is whether these changes appear to affect who runs, as the theory predicts they should. Chapters 5 and 6 offer analyses that suggest the answer is yes.

CHAPTER FIVE

Depolarization and the
Benefits of Office

In this chapter, I show evidence in favor of a key prediction of this book's argument: when the benefits of holding office increase, a more-moderate set of people run for office and legislatures appear to become less polarized.

First, to explain the idea and give it context, I conduct a case study of Alaska, which implemented a dramatic salary increase for state legislators in 2010. The commission that recommended the increase specifically discussed the issue of encouraging candidates to run for office. In the aftermath of the increase, which more than doubled salaries, the set of people who ran for the Alaska state legislature became considerably less polarized.

Next, I perform a larger-scale statistical analysis. I collect new data on salaries in state legislatures since 1992. Comparing changes in who runs for office in states that increase their salaries to changes in other states that do not, I show that salary increases appear to encourage more moderate people to run for the state legislatures. Although the results are less precise, I also show evidence that higher salaries lead legislatures to become less polarized, on average. These latter findings are important because they suggest that when more moderates run for office—as when they are encouraged to run because of higher salaries—they are able to win office, as would be predicted by the results in chapter 3.

Separate from studying salaries, I also examine how the candidate pool changes when the expected benefits of holding office decrease because the chance of winning goes down. I compare the ideologies of the people who run for office when they can do so for an open seat, when winning is more probable, versus when an incumbent holds the seat, which makes winning extremely difficult. The set of people who run against incumbents is more ideologically extreme, on average, than the set of those who run for open seats. Again, this finding is consistent with the theoretical prediction that lower expected benefits of office should discourage more-moderate candidates from running.

I conclude the chapter by relating these analyses back to the theoretical argument presented in chapter 1. A key prediction of the theory is that more-moderate people will be more willing to run for office when the benefits of winning office are higher. Although it is impossible to measure the benefits of office fully, the analyses in this chapter study important components of these overall benefits and consistently find that higher benefits encourage more-moderate people to run for office. Since I have argued that the benefits of holding office in the U.S. House have gone down, this evidence suggests that the decline in the benefits of office may help explain the rising polarization of who runs for office and of legislative polarization in the House.

Higher Legislative Salaries Encourage Moderates

In this section, I study salary increases in state legislatures and show that they lead to more-moderate candidate pools and less-polarized legislatures, in line with the theoretical predictions from chapter 1. It is impossible to study the effects of salaries at the federal level because they are the same across all members of the legislature—we have no way of plausibly comparing different contexts where salaries are high versus low to see how they affect who runs for office. This is why I pivot to studying the state legislatures in this section. Although state legislatures differ from the House in a variety of ways, they tell us a great deal about politics at the federal level. As I will explain later, a considerable number of members of the House come from state legislatures. Moreover, a number of studies show how politics in the state legislatures teaches us about legislatures more generally (see, e.g., Barber 2015; Fouirnaies and Hall 2018; Shor and McCarty 2011; Squire 2012).

Why Salaries Are a Useful Type of Office Benefit to Study

Many of the most important benefits of holding political office—such as the chance to influence policy, the burnished reputation of being a public servant, and the opportunity to hold lucrative positions after retiring from political office (all discussed in chapter 4)—are difficult to measure with data. Legislator salaries, however, are an important and observable type of benefit, and that is why I focus on salaries in this section.

Previous research shows the value of studying politician pay. Besley (2004) offers a theoretical framework for thinking about how politician pay influences both the set of people who run for office and the behavior of those who win office. Studying U.S. governors, Besley shows that governors in states and times where salaries are higher are ideologically more congruent with their constituents than are governors in states and times where salaries are lower—a similar pattern to what I document for the state legislatures in this chapter. In a similar vein, Gagliarducci and Nannicini (2013) show that higher salaries in Italian municipal governments encourage people with higher levels of education to run for—and win— political office. Finally, Dal Bó, Finan, and Rossi (2013) show results from a randomized experiment in Mexico in which higher salaries attracted people with more relevant work experience, higher intelligence scores, and better personality traits, to apply for public office. In sum, this political economy literature suggests that, while there are many other forms of office benefits, salary is an important component worth studying.

Data and Background on State Legislative Salaries

To evaluate whether higher salaries encourage more-moderate candidates to run for office, I collected a new data set on salaries for legislators in the fifty states. The data come from the *Book of the States* (Council of State Governments 2018) and cover the years 1992–2012 once merged with the campaign finance data.

Salaries vary widely across the states, not only in their magnitude but also in their form. Most states offer a fixed salary to legislators, sometimes with modest pay raises for those holding leadership positions. These salaries are typically set equal for state senators and members of the state house. Some states instead pay legislators a set rate per day the legislature is in session. For these latter states, I multiply their daily wage by the average number of days the legislature is in session (another piece of data available in the *Book of the States*).

Figure 5.1 presents the salaries of the state legislators as of 2012. As the bar graph shows, there is tremendous variation. California leads the pack, paying legislators an annual salary of almost $100,000. Pennsylvania, New

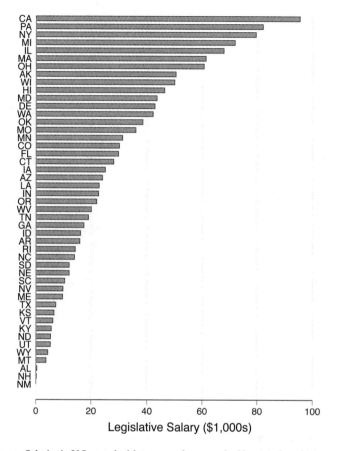

FIGURE 5.1. Salaries in U.S. state legislatures as of 2012, ranked by state from highest to lowest. *Note*: Salary data from *Book of the States* (Council of State Governments 2018).

York, and Michigan are not far behind. In contrast, at the bottom of the graph, Alabama and New Hampshire pay their legislators almost nothing, while New Mexico actually pays its legislators literally nothing. (New Mexican state legislators are, however, entitled to a per diem intended to reimburse expenses incurred in the course of their political duties.)

Despite this variation, making a raw comparison of the ideology of those who run for office when salaries are high versus when salaries are low would not tell us much about whether raising salaries induces moderates to run. Obvious forms of selection bias lurk. Wealthier states with more active business communities, for example, might have a more-moderate candidate pool and pay legislators more, producing a spurious correlation between the two variables. To deal with this issue, I again turn to a difference-in-differences design. I compare *changes* in the ideology of the candidate pool before and after states change how much they pay their legislators to changes in other states with no salary reforms over the same period.

How, when, and why do states change the salaries of their legislators? States have various mechanisms by which they can change these salaries, but most commonly either the legislature passes a bill to change its own pay, or an independent commission chooses a new salary level for members of government. Since 1990, when the data start, we observe forty-nine distinct salary reforms. These reforms range in size from a roughly $300 annual increase, in Wyoming in 1992, to a $26,000 annual increase passed in Alaska in 2010. From a research perspective, the main concern is whether these changes occur strategically. If they do, even the difference-in-differences design may attribute effects of these strategically timed reforms improperly. However, as I show in the following case study, standard validity checks suggest that this strategic aspect is not a problem, probably because salary changes most often are imposed on the legislature externally.

Alaska's Legislative Salary Increase: A Case Study

The largest state legislative salary increase in recent times took place in Alaska in 2010. The State of Alaska appointed an independent commission to review salaries for government officials, recognizing that it was politically infeasible for elected officials to set their own salaries in the current political climate. The commission weighed many of the same issues I have discussed in this book. Speaking generally, the commission's report read:

> Public service has non-monetary compensation. For some commissioners, public service represents a form of repayment to society for the opportunities it has provided them to achieve success and prosperity. For some it has the rewards of shaping public policies about which they have strong feelings. But along with its rewards, public service also entails costs, such as the loss of privacy, exposure to public criticism, possible relocation to the capital, and interruption of a career. It many also involve financial loss, both because of a lower salary and because of conflict-of-interest regulations that require divestiture of certain assets. To make cabinet posts as attractive as possible, salary levels have to be commensurate with the heavy responsibilities of office and also reasonably competitive with private-sector employment. Members of the commission believe it is

necessary to increase the salaries of department heads to make service in the governor's cabinet as attractive and feasible for as many people as possible.[1]

Later in the report, the commission turned specifically to the issue of legislator salaries:

When a generally low and ambiguous system of compensation is combined with the large commitment of time required by legislative service, the disruption of careers and family life that it often entails, the increasing use of special sessions called at all times of the year, the general decline of remunerative seasonal employment, and the increasingly stringent ethics regulations that foreclose many business opportunities for self-employed attorneys and other professional people, legislative service is not an attractive or even realistic prospect for many people. Consequently, the legislature does not represent a cross section of the Alaska public in terms of age, gender, and socioeconomic characteristics. It is heavily weighted with older, retired individuals, and those who are financially independent or without family obligations.

Legislators have the responsibility for decisions of momentous importance for Alaska and its citizens. The Alaska Legislature is a branch of government co-equal with the executive and judiciary, and it deserves all of the dignity and respect properly due the other branches. The current system of compensating Alaskans who serve in the legislature is unworthy of the farreaching duties and responsibilities inherent in the institution of the legislature.[2]

Based on this logic, the commission doubled the salaries of Alaskan legislators, from roughly \$24,000 to just over \$50,000.[3] How do these increases affect who runs for office?

To measure the polarization of the candidate pool, I calculate the estimated ideological difference between each candidate and the median candidate across both parties running for the same office at the same time. For example, for a candidate running for state senate in Alaska in 2012, I calculate the distance between that candidate's CFScore and the median CFScore for all candidates running for Alaska's state senate in 2012. I then take the average distance—that is, averaging over all candidates' distances—as the measure of candidate-pool polarization for Alaska's state senate in 2012.

To start, I perform a simple case study of Alaska's change, using the technique of synthetic control (Abadie, Diamond, and Hainmueller 2010) to find a hypothetical control state that looks just like Alaska, in terms of

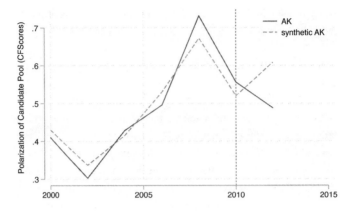

FIGURE 5.2. Moderating effect of Alaska's increase in state legislator salaries. This line plot shows the polarization of candidates running for the Alaska Legislature, over time, compared to a synthetic control version of Alaska. Alaska's large salary increase, put into place in 2010, appears to have substantially reduced polarization in the candidate pool in 2012.

its candidate polarization in the years before Alaska's salary reform, but that does not initiate a salary reform. Because the reform was relatively recent, Alaska offers a good number of preintervention years, which are necessary to find an effective synthetic control.[4] Figure 5.2 shows the time trends for Alaska (AK) compared with its control (synthetic AK), before and after the 2010 reform.

As the figure shows, the synthetic version of Alaska looks much like it, in terms of candidate-pool polarization, before the reform in 2010. After the salary increase, though, the real Alaska's candidate pool appears to become significantly less polarized. In 2012, the average distance from the median candidate, in terms of CFScores, is roughly 0.12 points lower in Alaska than it is in the hypothetical version of Alaska without the salary increase. Though it is hard to interpret the size of this effect substantively, it is almost exactly half a standard deviation in the candidate-pool polarization measure, across all states, and roughly equal to the within-state standard deviation in this measure (0.11). I will discuss other ways to interpret the estimated effect in the following section. Generally speaking, the effects of large salary increases seem to be meaningful and detectable.

The Effect of Salary Increases: Full Analysis

To estimate the overall effect of salary increases on who runs for office, I focus on comparing how states' candidate pools change after salary increases to changes in candidate pools over the same period in states that do not implement salary increases. Even when performing an analysis that focuses on within-state variation in salaries, we might worry that other differences besides changing salaries are driving the results. In particular, within states, a main driver of salary changes is inflation. That is, if we measure salaries in real dollars, then most of the changes from year to year in legislator salaries come from changes in the value of a dollar, rather than from actual reforms in how much they are paid. This variation is unlikely to be helpful since such changes are occurring simultaneously in any of the other jobs would-be legislators might take instead. To deal with this issue, I instead perform the analysis using nominal dollars. This way, the only time legislator salaries change in the data is when a state actually chooses to change legislator salaries.

Figure 5.3 presents the main result. The scatterplot compares the polarization of the candidate pool to the logged salaries state legislators receive across states and time. Points in the plot are binned averages of candidate-pool polarization, where the sizes of the bins are chosen to make the sample size in each bin equal. Points are also first residualized by state and year so that the graph reflects the difference-in-differences design; the reader can think about the resulting relationship being causal,

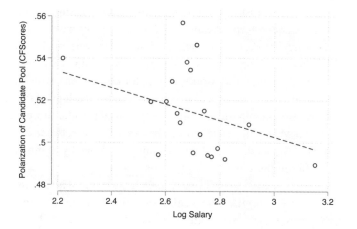

FIGURE 5.3. Legislator salaries and candidate ideologies in state legislatures, 1990–2012. This scatterplot shows that when states increase legislator salaries, the candidate pool becomes less polarized. *Note*: Polarization is measured as the average absolute distance in CFscore ideology between each candidate and the median candidate for a given office. Points are averages in equal-sample-sized bins of the log salary variable. Points are residualized by state and year to reflect difference-in-differences design.

so long as the key assumption from the difference-in-differences design is met—that is, that the states that do not have salary changes provide a useful counterfactual representation for how the pool of candidates in a state that did change its salary would have changed over time if it hadn't changed its salary.

As the figure shows, when states increase legislator salaries, the candidate pool becomes noticeably less polarized. Consider first the leftmost point on the plot. This point is an average of all the years in all states where the annual salary in nominal dollars was around ten thousand dollars (so that logged thousands of dollars is around 2.2). For these cases, as we see, the candidate pool is most polarized, with the average distance between candidates and the median competitor at roughly 0.54 on the CFScore scale. As we follow the plot to the right, as salaries increase, we see observations containing races with increasingly less polarized candidate pools. Though these cases are still quite polarized, the decrease is apparent.

As the accompanying table shows (see table A3.1 in appendix 3), an increase from the smallest to the largest observed salary is estimated to reduce the polarization of the candidate pool by 0.345 points on the CFScore scale.

Is this a substantively meaningful decrease? One way to think about this is to compare candidates who are roughly 0.345 points away in the CFScore measure from each other, to get a sense for what kind of gap this is. In 2014, this distance is roughly equal to the estimated ideological distance between Republicans Paul Ryan, the conservative, business-oriented future Speaker, and Michelle Bachmann, one of the most extreme members of Congress in recent times. The ideological gap between them seems larger than one would expect for copartisans, which in turn suggests that the effect of increasing salaries on the ideology of the candidate pool is also meaningful. A big increase in salary, like those enacted in Alaska and Michigan, could shrink the average gap between any given candidate and the median candidate running for office by as much as the distance between these two distinct legislators.

Another way to figure out if this change is meaningful is to consider its downstream effects on the polarization of sitting legislators. If the candidate pool becomes more moderate after salaries increase, and if voters prefer more moderate candidates, then we should see the legislature become less polarized.

Figure 5.4 presents the same analysis now using the polarization of the legislature, measured using the Shor and McCarty NP-Scores based on

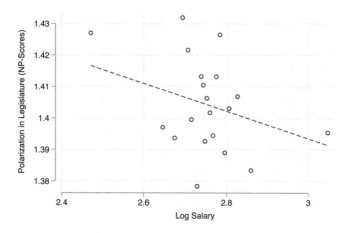

FIGURE 5.4. Legislator salaries and polarization in state legislatures, 1990–2012. This scatter-plot shows that when states increase legislator salaries, the legislature becomes less polarized. *Note*: Polarization is measured as the average absolute distance between the party medians in the legislature. Points are averages in equal-sample-sized bins of the log salary variable. Points are residualized by state and year to reflect difference-in-differences design.

state legislative roll-call votes (Shor and McCarty 2011). We see a similar decrease. As predicted, when states raise legislative salaries, legislative polarization goes down. It is important to highlight that these results are not as statistically precise as those estimated on the candidate pool (see table A3.2 in appendix 3 for more details). Nevertheless, the pattern is consistent with the results on the candidate pool and with the theoretical predictions.

To assess the impact of this effect, we can again consider the effect if we go from the lowest to the highest salary. This is estimated to decrease legislative polarization by roughly 0.3 on the NP-Score scale. It is difficult to know what this means, but given that the within-state standard deviation in NP-Score polarization is 0.13, a decrease of 0.3 represents more than a two-standard-deviation decrease in polarization—which suggests that it is a large effect.

Salaries and Depolarization

In this section, I have used a case study and a large-scale statistical analysis to show how increases in state legislative salaries encourage moderates to run for office and, as a result, appear to depolarize legislatures. Although these latter findings are tentative, they are especially noteworthy for this book's argument. I have argued that the entry of more-moderate candidates would lower polarization in the U.S. House. The evidence for this claim, offered in chapter 3, is only indirect; it establishes that, among the candidates who have chosen to run for the House, those who are more moderate do better, electorally. What those analyses do not say is whether *new* House candidates who hold more-moderate positions would *also* do better than more-extreme candidates, electorally. The evidence in this chapter on state legislative polarization suggests the answer is yes. If higher state legislative salaries both encourage greater numbers of moderate people to run for office *and* lead to lower levels of legislative polarization, then it is plausible that new moderate candidates also do well, electorally.

Incumbents and the Scare-Off of Moderates

In this section, I study changes not in the benefits of office, directly, but in the probability that a candidate will be able to enjoy the benefits of office. Specifically, I show that when U.S. House seats are held by incumbents, candidates in the *out party*—that is, the party that does not hold the seat—are more extreme, on average. This is further indirect evidence that more-moderate candidates are more likely to run for office when the benefits of office are higher.

The analysis in the previous section on salaries has the advantage of examining a tractable, quantitative measure of a tangible benefit to holding office. However, it is possible that candidates deciding to run for state legislatures are fundamentally different than those who run for the U.S. House. In addition, we might worry that salary is only a small factor in the benefits that would-be candidates for the House are considering. Accordingly, in this section I focus specifically on the House, and I scrutinize a different kind of benefit.

Specifically, I take advantage of the fact that it is difficult to challenge incumbents in the U.S. House (e.g., Jacobson 2012). When an incumbent holds a seat, challengers in the other party have a minimal chance of winning office—as such, incumbents can be thought of as reducing the expected benefits of office for would-be candidates. To see how much this factor changes the ideological composition of the candidate pool, I compare who runs for office to challenge an incumbent with who runs for office in open-seat races.

Main Results: Candidates More Extreme
When Chance of Winning Is Lower

Figure 5.5 offers an overview of the results. The figure plots the average ideological positions of the candidates who run for office in three mutually exclusive cases: when the seat is held by a Republican incumbent; when the seat is open; and when the seat is held by a Democratic incumbent. The circles indicate the average ideology of Democratic candidates, across all races; the squares represent the average ideology of Republican candidates.

Consider the circles on the left side of the figure. The top circle shows that when there is a Republican incumbent, the set of Democrats who run for office is particularly left-wing, on average; when the seat is open, as shown by the middle circle, they are more moderate, on average; and in the seats that Democrats hold, the pool (including the incumbent), represented by the bottom circle, is the most moderate of all the three cases.

The same pattern holds for Republicans, shown by squares on the right side of the figure. When the seat is held by a Republican incumbent, as indicated by the top square, the set of Republicans who run for office is the most moderate of the three candidate pools; Republican candidates for open-seat races are less moderate, on average; and Republican candidates

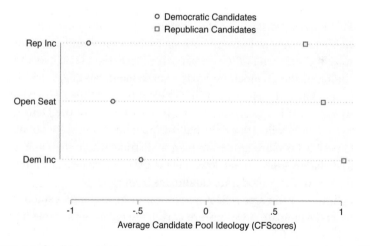

FIGURE 5.5. Candidate-pool ideology with and without incumbents seeking reelection, U.S. House of Representatives, 1980–2012. The circles indicate the average ideology of Democratic candidates, across all races; the squares represent the average ideology of Republican candidates. Both parties field more ideologically extreme candidates, on average, in seats held by the other party.

for seats held by Democrats are the most right-wing, on average. It appears that the set of people who run for office is more extreme in cases where the expected benefits of office are lower.

Formal Results

I now turn to more formal results, briefly. The analysis I just presented is clear, but it could fall victim to biases if the sets of districts with Republican incumbents, with Democratic incumbents, and with no incumbents are systematically different from each other in ways that affect who runs for office. The most obvious concern is that seats with a Republican incumbent will be in more right-wing areas (and vice versa for Democratic seats)—but this should bias the analysis away from finding differences in the candidate pools, because we would think that would make Democratic candidates in Republican-held areas more right-wing, too.

To address these kinds of issues, we need a technique to hold fixed the underlying characteristics of the districts. I again turn to a regression discontinuity design, like the one used in chapter 3, to accomplish this goal. Specifically, I compare subsequent candidate pools in districts that just barely elect a Democratic candidate to districts that just barely elect a Republican candidate.

Figure 5.6 shows the results of one of these analyses graphically, using the Democratic Party as the example. The horizontal axis reflects the winning margin, in terms of vote share, for Democratic candidates in elections at time t, while the vertical axis reflects the average ideological positioning of the Democratic Party's subsequent candidate pool—that is, all candidates who enter the primary election—at time $t + 1$ (typically, the primary election two years later). In districts where the Democratic candidate barely wins (the right half of the figure), the subsequent candidate pool is far more moderate than in districts where the Democratic candidate barely loses. Again, lowering the expected chance of winning office appears to deter moderate candidates from running.

Might these estimates reflect a scare-off of high-quality candidates, if quality and candidate positions are correlated? This is certainly a possibility. However, for the same set of races—close elections in the U.S. House—I find that there is almost no scare-off of candidates with previous officeholder experience (Hall and Snyder, 2015b). Thus the effects observed here are likely to be driven, at least largely, by ideology.

Challenging an incumbent of the other party is an uphill battle in the

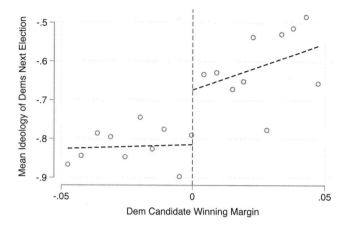

FIGURE 5.6. Incumbency and the ideology of subsequent candidates, U.S. House of Representatives, 1980–2012. The candidate pool is more extreme after elections in which the other party barely wins office (left of discontinuity) than after elections in which the party barely wins office (right of discontinuity). The figure uses the Democratic Party as the reference party, but results are essentially identical when focusing on the Republican Party instead.

U.S. House. Whereas it may or may not require higher costs than does running in an open seat, it almost certainly represents, on average, a decrease in expected benefits for would-be candidates. In this section, I have explored this effect to learn about how changes in the expected benefits of office affect who runs for office. When a coin flip gives one party control of a U.S. House seat, the other party's subsequent candidates in that district become more ideologically extreme than in the counterfactual scenario where it won the seat instead. Consistent with the predictions of the theory I laid out in chapter 1, the set of people who run is more moderate when expected benefits are higher, and it is more extreme when they are lower.

Summary: Greater Benefits of Office Encourage Moderates and Depolarize Legislatures

I began this book by showing why considering who runs for office is important for understanding polarization in the U.S. House. The majority of legislative polarization in the House does not appear to be due to the choices voters make in elections, but is already inherent in the set of candidates who run for office. I then offered a theoretical argument that highlighted how the costs and benefits of seeking office can disproportionately deter moderate people from becoming candidates. In this chapter, I have offered empirical evidence consistent with this claim. Studying both state legislatures and the U.S. House, I have shown statistical evidence that when the benefits of holding office rise, the set of people who run for office becomes more moderate.

CHAPTER SIX

Polarization and the Costs of Running

In the last chapter, I offered evidence that higher benefits of holding office lead to more-moderate people running for office. Now, in the final empirical chapter of the book, I turn to the question of whether costs of running for office have a similar effect on the candidate pool, as the book's theory predicts. Focusing on state legislators, I offer some preliminary evidence that those who have compiled more ideologically extreme records are not only more likely to run for the House (as shown in Thomsen 2017) but remain more likely to do so even when they must give up their state legislative seat to run. More-moderate state legislators, on the other hand, are more sensitive to this cost. These results are less strong, statistically speaking, than the results in previous chapters, reflecting in large part the fundamental empirical challenges of studying the largely unobserved costs of running for office. Nonetheless, they are quite suggestive and are in line with the theory's predictions.

Ideology and Running for the House: Two Contrasting Cases

In 2002, Alice Kerr was a state senator serving Kentucky's twelfth state senatorial district, a job she had held since 1998. In her time in the state senate, Kerr, a Republican, had amassed a policy portfolio that was classified as moderate when considered in relation to her peers in the legislature. Based on her roll-call votes in the Shor and McCarty (2011) database, Kerr was markedly left of the Republican Party's median legislator, though to the right of the state legislature's overall median legislator. Given her experience and visibility in the state senate, one might suspect that Kerr had her eye on Kentucky's Sixth Congressional District, her home district, but as of 2004 Kerr had never chosen to make a bid for federal office. No doubt, there are many possible reasons Kerr had not yet tried for the U.S. House, including the fact that the Sixth District seat was at that time held by physician and popular politician Ernie Fletcher, also a Republican. But it may have also entered Kerr's mind that to run would entail special risks for her. As in most states, in Kentucky candidates cannot run for a new office while simultaneously seeking reelection for their current office.[1] If she were to run for the U.S. House, Kerr, like most other state legislators, would have to make the difficult decision to surrender her current political office. If her campaign were unsuccessful, she would be left without either job.

Then, fortune struck. In December 2002, Fletcher announced that he would run for governor. In Kentucky, gubernatorial elections occur separately from legislative elections—meaning that when Fletcher went on to win the governorship, there was a special election, held at its own special time, to replace his seat in the House. Kerr could seek out this seat without surrendering her current office. Only then did Kerr enter the race for U.S. House; she went on to win the Republican primary but lose the general election, returning to her state senate seat, which she still held as of mid-2018. In March 2016, Kerr joined four other state senate Republicans in crossing party lines to vote against Kentucky's controversial SB 180, a bill that would have made a legal allowance for business owners to refuse to serve gay customers on religious grounds (Brammer 2016). In the years since her failed U.S. House bid, Kerr continued to compile a reliably moderate record as she rose through the ranks of the state senate.

The electoral story of Alice Kerr is a relatively common one in American politics. Lyndon Johnson famously made his first attempt for the U.S. Senate in a special election which allowed him to run without having to give up his current office—a good thing for Johnson, since he narrowly lost the election to W. L. "Pappy" O'Daniel, the popular radio host and political firebrand. Johnson was able to lick his political wounds from the comfort of his office in the House, and he went on to win a Senate seat on his next try (though not without controversy). As I will document later in this chapter, politicians are, perhaps not surprisingly, sensitive to the cost of giving up a certain job for the uncertain prospect of a different one. But what is perhaps more surprising—but consistent with the theoretical argument I have outlined—is that this sensitivity varies across the ideological spectrum.

Consider now the case of Rep. Tom McClintock (R-CA), who as of mid-2018 represented California's Fourth Congressional District. A Republican,

McClintock ranked as one of the most far right-wing state legislators ever to serve in any state legislature when he was in the California state legislature, according to the Shor and McCarty (2011) data. McClintock gave up his seat in the state legislature not once but twice to run for the House—first in 1992, when he was a member of the California State Assembly, and then again in 2008, when he was a state senator. In the interim, he ran for—and sometimes, but not usually, won—a dizzying array of offices. After ten years in the State Assembly, followed by an unsuccessful bid for the U.S. House, McClintock ran for state controller twice (both times without success), for governor twice (both times without success), and for state senate (successfully). When he finally made it to the U.S. House after giving up his state senate seat in 2008, McClintock joined the so-called Freedom Caucus, the Tea Party–affiliated group that famously opposed Speaker John Boehner and generally represented the Republican Party's farthest right flank.

Needless to say, Alice Kerr and Tom McClintock are just two examples pulled from the vast sea of people who have seen fit to run for Congress. But, as the following analyses will suggest, their stories may be telling. While more moderate individuals are more careful about running for office, and are more sensitive to the many costs of candidacy, more ideologically extreme individuals are more likely to commit to running, whatever the costs.

State Senators and Running for the House

State legislators represent an important swath of the overall candidate supply. Candidates with state legislative experience outperform inexperienced candidates in U.S. House elections (e.g., Jacobson 1989), and roughly 28 percent of all U.S. House candidates, 1980–2010, were previously state legislators.[2] As a result, while focusing on state legislators for this test inevitably narrows its applicability, the results of the test speak directly to some of the most viable members of the candidate supply and likely generalize to others, too. The idea to investigate the candidate pool by looking at state legislators is not novel and has been fruitfully executed in the past. Maestas et al. (2006, 196) report that state legislators "have provided the dominant path to the U.S. House." Using novel survey data, the authors argue that state legislators follow a two-step process in determining their future political careers, first choosing whether to run, and then, conditional on this

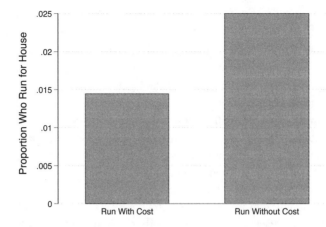

FIGURE 6.1. Comparison between state senators who run for the U.S. House of Representatives when they would incur the cost of surrendering their current seat and those who would run without that cost. State senators are more likely to run for the House when they do not have to give up their current seat.

decision, choosing *when* to run. More recently, and more closely related to this analysis, Thomsen (2014, 2017) documents the finding that more ideologically extreme state legislators are more likely to run for office than are more-moderate state legislators.

Here, I investigate whether state legislators are more likely to make the leap to the U.S. House when they can run *without surrendering their state legislative seat.* In most cases, running for the House requires surrendering one's state legislative seat because the elections occur simultaneously and most states do not allow candidates to be listed on the ballot for multiple offices at the same time. However, state senators serving four-year terms have opportunities to run for the House in a year in which they do not have to defend their seat, allowing them to run without risking their current seat.

First, I verify that state senators are, in general, responsive to the costs of running for office. Figure 6.1 presents a simple comparison between state legislators in most times and places, who must give up their seat to run, and those lucky few who have a chance to run without giving up their seat. Roughly 1.4 percent of state legislators run for the House when they have to give up their seat to do so; but roughly 2.5 percent run when they can do so without giving up their seat—a proportional increase of nearly 80 percent. In appendix 4, I confirm these differences in a more formal regression analysis.

More-Extreme State Senators Less Sensitive to Costs

Although state legislators are, by and large, unlikely to run for the U.S. House, they are much more likely—almost twice as likely—to do so when the costs of doing so are lower. Candidates thus appear sensitive to the costs of running for office. Does this relationship vary with ideology, as my theory predicts?

To answer this question, I measure the gap between how often state senators run for the House when they can so without cost (without giving up their current seat) versus with cost (when they have to give up their current seat). I then compare the size of this gap across the ideological spectrum, measuring the ideological positions of state senators using their roll-call records (NP-Scores) and also using their campaign contributions (CFScores), the two main measures of ideology I have used throughout the book. If the costs of running for office disproportionately deter more-moderate people from running, as my theory predicts, then this gap should be larger for more-moderate state senators and smaller for more-extreme state senators.

Figure 6.2 suggests that this is indeed the case. Each point on the graph reflects the average rate at which a group of state senators who share similar NP-Scores chose to run for the U.S. House. These points are shaped to indicate whether these state senators were facing an opportunity to run that included paying the cost of giving up their current seat (circles) or an opportunity to run without that cost (squares). I add regression lines, fit separately for the with-cost and without-cost cases, to the scatterplot. On the left side of the graph, where we look at more-moderate state legislators, we see that the gap between the lines is large—that is, having the chance to run without cost increases the propensity of moderate state senators to run for the House by a large amount. Indeed, at the leftmost end of the graph, the gap is very large. Here, we estimate that the most moderate state senator runs for the House only about 1 percent of the time if he or she has to give up the current seat to do so; but the state senator runs almost 2.5 percent of the time if he or she can do so without giving up the current seat. This difference represents a 150 percent increase in the rate of running.

As we look to the right side of the graph, we see that this gap nearly goes away. For more-extreme state senators, there is less and less difference in the probability they run for the U.S. House when they have to pay the cost of surrendering their current seat versus when they do not. This cost of running for office does not appear to deter more-extreme state senators the way it deters more-moderate ones.

Figure 6.3 presents these results another way, measuring candidate ideology using CFScores instead of NP-Scores. Here, extremism is measured as the absolute distance from each state senator to the median member of his or her party seeking state senatorial office in a given year. Again, we find the same pattern. More-moderate state senators are much more likely to run when they can avoid the cost of surrendering their current seat than when they have to pay it, while more-extreme state senators are far less sensitive to this cost.

In appendix 4, I offer some attempts to estimate these patterns formally. As the estimates show, while the differences between more-moderate and more-extreme state senators are large, it is difficult to rule out the possibil-

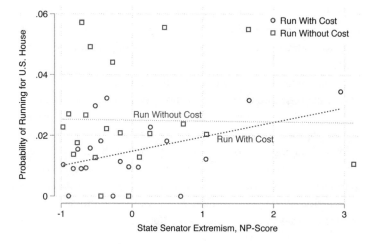

FIGURE 6.2. Evidence from state legislators running for the U.S. House of Representatives that costs of running deter moderate candidates, using NP-Scores. This graph plots the relationship between extremism, measured with NP-Scores, and the propensity to run for the U.S. House for state legislators, 1994–2012, for two sets of cases: when a state legislator must give up the current seat to run for the House ("Run With Cost"); and when the state legislator does not need to give up the current seat to run ("Run Without Cost"). To the left side of the graph, we see a big gap between the propensity to run and the cost; more-moderate legislators are much more likely to run if the they can do so without this cost. To the right side of the graph, we see that this gap all but disappears for more-extreme state legislators. *Note:* Points are averages in equal-sample-sized bins of state senator extremism. Extremism is measured as the absolute distance in NP-Score ideology between each legislator and the median member of the legislator's party, in the state legislature, in each year. Plot generated using Stata binscatter command.

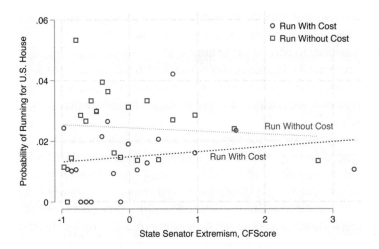

FIGURE 6.3. Evidence from state legislators running for the U.S. House that costs of running deter moderate candidates, using CFscores. This graph plots the relationship between extremism, measured with CFscores, and the propensity to run for the U.S. House for state legislators, 1994–2012, for two sets of cases: when a state legislator must give up the current seat to run for the house ("Run With Cost"); and when the state legislator does not need to give up the current seat to run ("Run Without Cost"). To the left side of the graph, we see a big gap between the propensity to run and the cost; more-moderate legislators are much more likely to run if the they can do so without this cost. To the right side of the graph, we see that this gap all but disappears for more-extreme state legislators. *Note*: Points are averages in equal-sample-sized bins of state senator extremism. Extremism is measured as the absolute distance in CFscore ideology between each legislator and the median member of the legislator's party, in the state legislature, in each year. Plot generated using Stata binscatter command.

ity that they are the result of statistical chance. Because so many state senators never run for the U.S. House, it is difficult to estimate these effects precisely. Although the graphical evidence I have offered here is extremely suggestive, it is important to bear in mind that this evidence is preliminary in nature. I leave it to future work to define and measure additional dimensions of the costs of running for office, so that the theory's prediction can be tested in other contexts with other, more powerful methods.

Summary: Costs and the Decision to Run for Office

This chapter has established two important facts about how candidates decide to run for office. First, they are, on average, sensitive to the costs of running. When state senators can run for the U.S. House without giving up their current seat, they are more than twice as likely to do so. Not surprisingly, would-be candidates are sensitive to how costly it is to run. Second, this sensitivity to costs does not appear to be constant across the ideological spectrum. As predicted, more-moderate potential candidates appear to be more sensitive to the costs of running—that is, they are more easily deterred by higher costs—than are more ideologically extreme would-be candidates.

As chapter 1 established, to understand polarization in the U.S. House, we need to understand who runs for office. I have argued that the rising costs of running for office are one of the important reasons that the set of people who run for the House has become more ideologically polarized over time, polarizing the House itself in turn. There are many costs to running for office, and the modest analysis in this chapter barely scratches the surface. Nevertheless, focusing on state senators, I have found suggestive evidence in favor of my theory's prediction. When it comes to giving up one's current job—a major cost to would-be candidates—more-moderate state senators appear to be more sensitive to the cost than are more-extreme state senators. This differential sensitivity, consistent with the theoretical predictions from chapter 1, suggests that the rising costs and falling benefits of seeking political offices such as the U.S. House can lead to legislative polarization. Lowering the costs of running for office is thus a plausible way to encourage more-moderate people to run.

CONCLUSION

Who Wants to Run?
in Broader Context

The nature of the workings of government depends ultimately on the men [or women] who run
it. . . . Let there be emphasis on those we elect to office.— V. O. Key, *American State Politics:
An Introduction*

The ideological polarization of our legislatures is one of the major issues in contemporary American politics, and understanding its causes
is among the most-studied questions in contemporary political science.
The purpose of this book has been to show why the question "who wants
to run?" helps us understand the roots of this polarization. While most
research has focused on how voters drive polarization, I offered evidence
in chapter 1 that the bulk of legislative polarization is not the result of the
choices that voters make. Even if voters selected the most moderate available candidate in every election for the U.S. House of Representatives
in every year since 1980, there would still have been a dramatic rise in
polarization in the House. Quantitative data on the ideological platforms
of 24,123 candidates for the House since 1980 show that the set of people
who run for office has become significantly more ideologically extreme in
the late twentieth and early twenty-first centuries.

These patterns, in turn, prompted a theory of why some people run for
office while others do not. The theory I proposed in chapter 1 suggests
that the growing burdens of running for the House coupled with the declining benefits of being a member of the House have discouraged moderate people from seeking office. The result is that voters by and large have
no choice but to elect more-extreme citizens to be their representatives.

To support these arguments, I have also offered a variety of analyses
suggesting that changing the costs and benefits of office really does affect

who runs. When state legislatures pay legislators more, the candidate pool appears to become less polarized—and so do the legislatures themselves. When running for the House is more difficult because it requires challenging an incumbent, the candidate pool becomes more extreme, on average. And when state legislators can run for the House without giving up their current seat, a more moderate group steps forward. All of these analyses are only indirect—it is impossible to measure the full costs and benefits of running for the House, and therefore impossible to directly relate these costs and benefits to the candidate pool—but they all suggest that the theory captures something true about what drives people to run for office and about why these choices are uneven across the ideological spectrum today.

Reducing Polarization

Inevitably, the specific conditions of today's political environment drive the way we think about politics and the specific research questions we choose to ask. Just as I have focused in this book on polarization, political scholars of the mid-twentieth century focused on the *lack* of polarization in Congress (APSA Committee Report 1950). We must always be mindful of our tendency to become overfocused on what seems to be the crisis of the day.

As such, I do not wish to overemphasize the potential deleterious effects of our current legislative polarization. As I said in chapter 1, legislative polarization likely encourages legislative gridlock, and it also appears to be contrary to the wishes of voters. These are two main reasons I do think politics would be improved if legislative polarization were lower—a goal we might achieve if we could revalue political office. On the other hand, would-be reformers should always keep in mind the trade-offs inherent in any policy choices. Higher legislative salaries, to pick the most controversial example I've focused on, might well lower polarization—but, as many have argued, they might encourage corruption and increase the likelihood that we pick venal types for office (see discussion in Besley 2004). As Benjamin Franklin declared, "Place before the eyes of such men a post of honor, that shall, at the same time, be a place of profit, and they will move heaven and earth to obtain it."[1] There is no magical fix to any political issue.

Rather than justifying any specific reform, my hope is that this book helps guide those interested in reform to focus on new goals. Separate from factors that change the way voters' choices are mapped into electoral choices—things like gerrymandering and primary elections, which are so popular at the moment—reformers might do well to consider why it is so hard to convince many people to run for political office, and to think about ways we might make it easier.

That is not to say that people do not already think about who runs for office. On the contrary, there is tremendous political activity across the ideological spectrum geared toward candidate recruitment, as well as considerable scholarship on the topic (cited in chapter 1). But there is little systematic thought about how to reform our institutions so that convincing people to run for office is easier. Begging people to become candidates for office would be much easier if we attacked some of the factors, most notably campaign finance, that currently deter so many citizens from entering politics.

Movements across the ideological spectrum gain notoriety and traction by crafting arguments and proposing concrete policies. Ultimately, this rhetoric is meaningless without electoral victory. No political movement can succeed without its proponents holding office, and no one can hold office who does not run for it in the first place.

A Different Way of Thinking about Elections and Ideology

Beyond contributing directly to the study of polarization in the U.S. House, this book is also intended to offer a different way of thinking about how to study elections and ideology more generally. This approach differs in two main ways from most existing research on the subject. First, it emphasizes electoral selection (the tendency for elections to choose particular types of candidates for office) rather than ideological accountability (the notion that elections can force candidates to change their platforms to suit voters). Second, motivated by this attention to electoral selection, the approach eschews survey-based studies of individual voter opinion and instead focuses on the observed decisions of electorates as a whole.

A Focus on Candidate Types and Electoral Selection

A main argument in chapter 2 was that we should think about candidates as—in part—possessing fixed ideological types, rather than having fluid platforms they strategically adapt as they go. My earlier work (Hall 2015), extended and replicated in chapter 3 of this book, offers a clear example of how this approach works. I seek to answer the question of whether or not more-moderate candidates do better than more-extreme candidates in U.S. House elections, on average.

The dominant approach to studying ideology and elections in American politics, motivated by the median voter theorem, seeks to link *changes* in candidate platforms to changes in electoral success. The design I present instead looks at changes in what type of candidate—more moderate or more extreme—is nominated to run in the general election, not supposing that each particular candidate ever changes positions at all. Although these two types of evidence may seem similar, they are distinct conceptually.

Indeed, in the median voter theorem framework, nominating a candidate with a more extreme platform would have no effect on general-election vote share, because any candidate would simply become moderate in the general election. The fact that I instead find a large electoral penalty to nominating more-extreme candidates strongly suggests the value of focusing on candidate type and not only on the idea of strategically adopted candidate positions. When we think about candidates as having ideological types, it is obvious why who runs for office is important for understanding polarization. Who runs for office is irrelevant for polarization if anyone who runs can become moderate, but it matters a great deal if polarization only goes down when moderates run and win office.

In addition, the idea of candidates as ideological types can change how we think about many other questions in electoral politics, beyond just legislative polarization. Consider, for one example, research that correlates incumbent positions with measures of constituent preferences in an effort to measure what is sometimes called *democratic responsiveness* (e.g., Tausanovitch and Warshaw 2013, 2014). Although these correlations are often interpreted as reflecting the degree to which incumbents respond to the desires of constituents, they could equally indicate the tendency for electorates to choose ideological types that fit their ideological preferences. Separating the electoral selection of ideologically congruent types from ideological accountability (i.e., responsiveness)—a parallel exercise to work that attempts to separate selection from accountability when studying candidate quality and effort (e.g., Alt, Bueno de Mesquita, and Rose 2011; Besley and Case 1995)—seems like a promising avenue for future research on elections and ideology.

Methods for Studying Electoral Selection

My focus on electoral selection also led me to a particular set of techniques and methods that may be valuable for future empirical work on candidate ideology and elections. As I explained in chapter 2, to study whether or not electorates favor more-moderate candidates, we do not want to isolate the effect of ideology, and we do not want to focus on the specific policy views or partisanship of voters.

These considerations led me to prefer systematic analyses of the candidate pool and electoral outcomes, taking advantage of recent technological advances that give us the opportunity, for the first time, to study the ideological positions of virtually the entire set of people who run for office. These advances solve only half the problem, though. Even with detailed data on who runs for office, to study electoral selection, we also need to be able to hold the underlying ideological preferences of each district fixed. The methodological discussion in chapter 2 details the existing approaches that try to do so, makes clear the assumptions necessary for them to work, and lays out a new technique based on studying close primary elections.

The result of this work is the most comprehensive evidence to date that U.S. House electorates favor more moderate candidates, on average.

A Bottom-Up View of Political Parties

Although parties have not been a major focus of this book—indeed, the theory presented in chapter 1 does not even consider them—the question "who wants to run?" may be crucial for understanding how parties are organized.

First, my approach suggests that pundits who discuss the parties consciously adopting specific issue positions may be overestimating their power. Political parties in the United States are fundamentally at the mercy of who runs for office. The parties may be able to tweak various aspects of their own platforms, but they are fragile. The moment a set of candidates who offer different positions runs for office and wins, the "party" and its platform instantaneously change. *To understand how parties come to hold the positions they hold, we should spend more time thinking about who runs for office.*

The 2016 election is a good example of this idea. What if Donald Trump had decided not to run for office? Republican primary voters would have been faced with a choice between a number of relatively conventional candidates, leading in all likelihood to a more conventional nominee. The media, I suspect, would then have interpreted the resulting Republican platform as the conscious choice of "the party." Instead, Trump chose to run. Because he won the primary, his choice fundamentally altered the subsequent platform of the party. The Republican Party's current "platform" is the direct result of Trump's choice to run for office, and of the primary voters' choices to nominate him for office.

Second, my approach suggests a new way of thinking that helps revise existing political-science theories of "parties-in-the-legislature." Aldrich (1995) famously organizes the idea of parties-in-the-legislature around the strategic incentives of individual legislators, following in the tradition of Mayhew (1974). The general idea of all the theoretical accounts of parties-in-the-legislature is that members organize together because it is valuable for them to do so, either because it enhances their reelection chances or because it helps them move policy in directions they favor (Aldrich and Rohde 2001; Cox and McCubbins 2005, 2007). But the choices that members of the legislature make to burnish their own prospects may affect the decisions of fellow party members whether to run for office. For example, it may be rational for members of the legislature to encourage the existing system of campaign finance, because it advantages them financially (Fouirnaies and Hall 2014) and because it raises the costs of running for potential high-quality challengers—but this decision may also deter high-quality challengers of their own party from challenging members of the other party. As a result, the decisions that legislators make to shore up their own prospects in their own districts may hurt their party in other districts. This could be one reason why we do not observe an electoral advantage to parties narrowly holding majority-party status (Feigenbaum, Fouirnaies, and Hall 2017).

Parties cannot be victorious electorally without encouraging electable candidates to run for office. Although observers of politics understand the primacy of candidate recruitment, there are many opportunities to add it to existing theories of the political process, and work in this vein is likely to be fruitful in the future.

Attracting High-Quality Candidates

I will conclude with one broader thought about who wants to run for office. This book has studied ideological polarization because it is a pressing issue in American politics today, and because it is a tangible attribute of political candidates that we can measure and understand. However, the main point of this book—that our electoral and legislative institutions deter the types of citizens that voters most prefer from running for office—is much broader than ideology. Ideological polarization is a salient issue of the day, but it is entirely contingent on the current state of American politics and society. In other places and times, where politics is less organized around a single dimension of ideological conflict, there is likely to be less ideological polarization in who runs for office. But this does not mean that "who wants to run?" will not be a relevant question. Quite the contrary.

The more fundamental problem faced by all democracies, in all times and places, is to attract good people to become politicians. Under some definitions, *good* may or may not include ideologically moderate, but in almost any definition, *good* will include such qualities as competence, integrity, and efficiency. Whether you want small or big government, whether you are conservative or liberal, you need high-quality representatives to achieve your vision of what our politics should look like. We cannot have high-quality representatives unless high-quality citizens run for office, and high-quality citizens will not run for office unless they have the proper incentives to do so.

As a result, far more work in the study of democratic politics should ask the question: *who wants to run?*

Additional Results on Polarization and Who Runs

A s I discussed in chapter 1, the conclusion that most of legislative polarization is not the result of whom voters pick for office, and instead is baked into who runs for office, does not rely on the use of CFScores to scale candidates. To show this, I now reproduce figure 1.2 using DW-DIME scalings instead of CFScores. The DW-DIME scalings are intended to use the contributions to estimate candidates' roll-call-based measures of ideology as closely as possible, and as a result, they clearly address the concern that CFScores pick up partisanship rather than ideology. The DW-DIME scalings are discussed in more detail in chapter 2.

As figure A1.1 shows, we draw the same conclusion when we use DW-DIME. The vast majority of polarization would still remain even if voters chose the least extreme candidate in every U.S. House election.

I also replicate the simulation using Hall-Snyder scores, which, as a reminder, do not use any contributions made after a candidate becomes an incumbent. As figure A1.2 shows, we continue to find the same pattern. In this scaling, polarization is at a very high level but would remain high even if voters chose the most moderate possible candidates. It is worth noting that in this final graph, the growth in polarization over time seems less dramatic than in the previous graphs. Although it is true that the growth appears smaller using the Hall-Snyder scaling—perhaps because the Hall-Snyder scaling is simply noisier due to its conservative use of data—some of the slope's apparent modesty simply comes from how I have scaled the plot. Even with this more conservative scaling, polarization has still grown by 28 percent since 1980.

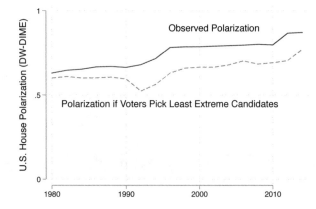

FIGURE A1.1. Legislative polarization not primarily explained by voter choices, 1980–2010, using DW-DIME. This graph compares observed legislative polarization, measured using DW-DIME, to the level of legislative polarization we would observe if in every district the most moderate (i.e., least extreme) candidate always won office. Because few moderates run for office, even if voters elected the most-moderate candidates who run, legislative polarization would still be very high.

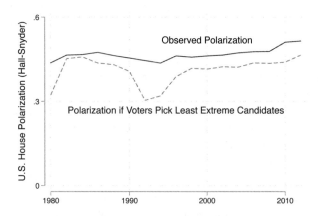

FIGURE A1.2. Legislative polarization not primarily explained by voter choices1980–2010, using Hall-Snyder. This graph compares observed legislative polarization, measured using Hall-Snyder scores, to the level of legislative polarization we would observe if in every district the most moderate (i.e., least extreme) candidate always won office. Because few moderates run for office, even if voters elected the most-moderate candidates who run, legislative polarization would still be very high.

A Formal Model of Who Wants to Run

I start by laying out the simple citizen-candidate model from Osborne and Slivinski (1996), with minor modifications. To be clear, this is not a model of my creating. In fact, much of my analysis comes from an undergraduate problem set question devised by Osborne (2004). But by going through it in detail, I can explain and defend my claim that increasing costs can lead to candidate divergence, which is not a focus of the original papers on the subject. Once I have done that, I can also modify the model to explore the consequences if moderates pay higher costs to run for office (or, similarly, if they face lower benefits of holding office).

Citizen i holds a unidimensional ideological position x_i. There is a continuum of citizens, and citizens are distributed across ideology according to the CDF F (where F is symmetric around the median). Citizens pay a cost c for sure if they choose to run; if citizen i wins office, he or she receives benefit b and implements policy $x^* = x_i$ for sure (consistent with the rigidity hypothesis from chapter 2). Citizen j who does not hold office receives payoff $-|x_j - x^*|$. The median citizen has position x_m. The utility for citizen i is

$$U_i(x^*) = \begin{cases} b - c & \text{if run and win} \\ -\left|x_i - x^*\right| - c & \text{if run and lose} \\ -\left|x_i - x^*\right| & \text{if don't run,} \end{cases}$$

where x^* is the ideal point of the winning candidate (so $x_i = x^*$ if i runs and wins). The game proceeds as follows. In the first stage, citizens simultaneously decide whether to run for office or not. Next, all citizens vote sincerely for the candidate closest to their ideal point. Finally, a candidate is selected as the winner, and that candidate's favored policy is implemented. Electoral ties are resolved by a fair coin flip, so if k candidates tie in an election, each has a $\frac{1}{k}$ chance of winning office.

Consider a proposed equilibrium in which two candidates, A and B, holding positions $x_m - \varepsilon$ and $x_m + \varepsilon$, run. Two main conditions must hold for this to be an equilibrium.[1]

Condition 1: Given that A and B run, the median citizen cannot run and win. For this to be true, it must be the case that the median citizen would receive fewer than one-third of the votes if he or she ran. Since the candidates must be arrayed symmetrically, this means that the leftmost candidates must be getting more than one-third of the votes. So, we must have

$$F\left(x_m - \frac{\varepsilon}{2}\right) \geq \frac{1}{3}$$

$$x_m - \frac{\varepsilon}{2} \geq F^{-1}\left(\frac{1}{3}\right)$$

$$\varepsilon \leq 2\left(F^{-1}\left(\frac{1}{2}\right) - F^{-1}\left(\frac{1}{3}\right)\right).$$

Condition 2: Neither A nor B can have incentive to drop out, given that other is running.

$$EU_1 \big| Run = \frac{1}{2}(b - c) + \frac{1}{2}(-c - 2\varepsilon)$$

$$EU_1 \big| NoRun = -2\varepsilon$$

$$\frac{1}{2}(b - c) + \frac{1}{2}(-c - 2\varepsilon) > -2\varepsilon$$

$$\frac{1}{2}b - c > -\varepsilon$$

$$\varepsilon > c - \frac{b}{2}.$$

Putting these together, we find the feasible range of ε such that we get a divergent, two-candidate equilibrium:

(A1.1) $$c - \frac{b}{2} < \varepsilon < 2\left(F^{-1}\left(\frac{1}{2}\right) - F^{-1}\left(\frac{1}{3}\right)\right).$$

Figure A1.3 depicts this equilibrium graphically.

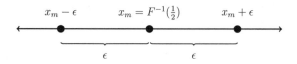

FIGURE A1.3. Divergence in two-candidate equilibria. This figure depicts equation A1.1 graphically.

Example with Uniform Distribution of Voters

Suppose $F: Unif(0,1)$, so that $x_m = \frac{1}{2}$. Using inequality A1.1, we now have the following bounds on ε:

(A1.2)
$$c - \frac{b}{2} < \varepsilon < \frac{1}{3}.$$

This means that the distance between each of the candidates and the median could be as much as one-third, which in turn would mean that fully two-thirds of all voters would be in between the positions of the two candidates. Graphically, we have the situation shown in figure A1.4. The middle point again shows the median. In the range just around the median, marked by the center curly bracket labeled "Cands Drop Out," there is no two-candidate equilibrium. In this region, $\varepsilon < c - \frac{b}{2}$, so that neither A nor B has an incentive to stay in the race given that the other is running.

Outside of this region, the next regions (one to each side) are those where two-candidate equilibria are possible. The labeled points to the left and right of the median, respectively, represent the positions A and B take in the maximally divergent equilibrium. In the uniform case, this divergence is quite large.

The final region toward each end of the spectrum again covers a case with no two-candidate equilibrium. Beyond $\frac{1}{6}$ and $\frac{5}{6}$, the positions become so extreme that a median candidate can enter and win outright, which such a candidate prefers to do.

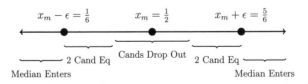

FIGURE A1.4. Divergence in two-candidate equilibria with a uniform distribution of voters. This figure depicts equation A1.2 graphically.

How Divergence Increases with Costs

Having fleshed out the basic model, we can now discuss how things change as costs, c, increase. Here we are dealing with a multitude of two-candidate equilibria defined by a range of feasible values ε can take on. As we increase c, we restrict this range. In particular, as we increase c, we rule out lower-divergence equilibria. If we refer back to equation A1.2 we can see why. Increases in c or decreases in b increase the lower bound that defines the set of values ε can take on in a two-candidate equilibrium. That is, the minimum distance away from the median citizen necessary to sustain a two-candidate equilibrium becomes larger when c increases or b decreases.

Why is this the case? The lower bound, $c - \dfrac{b}{2}$, reflects the willingness of the two candidates to pay the cost to run to avoid the ideological cost of dropping out and letting the opponent win and implement the opposition's policy. When we increase c or decrease b, we raise the costs of staying in the race while holding the ideological cost of dropping out and seeing the opponent implement the opposition's policy constant. Dropping out thus becomes increasingly attractive—in turn, the set of two-candidate equilibria contains only candidates who are farther away from the middle, far enough that they still fear the ideological cost of dropping out enough to stay in the race.

The claim that increases in c (or decreases in b) lead to greater divergence is therefore nuanced. It is not a traditional comparative static in the sense of saying "as we change this parameter, the equilibrium level of divergence changes as follows." Instead, the idea is that *only increasingly divergent equilibria (which are themselves unchanging) can be sustained as* c *increases or* b *decreases*. The important part is the intuition, though—I would not claim this model accurately reflects reality. But it captures the important point that, as it becomes more costly to run for office, or as it becomes less compelling to hold office, or both, races between two candidates become more divergent because more-moderate candidates aren't afraid enough of the ideological positions of their potential opponents to be willing to pay the cost to run.

We can also do a more traditional comparative static if we focus on the *least divergent* equilibrium, across values for c (or, equivalently, across values of b). The smallest ε that sustains a two-candidate equilibrium is always $c - \dfrac{b}{2}$. Thus, as c increases, *the least divergent two-candidate equilibrium becomes more divergent*.

Here's a formal way of stating that. Consider the set of two-candidate equilibria, $E = \{(\frac{1}{2} - \varepsilon, \frac{1}{2} + \varepsilon) : c - \frac{b}{2} \leq \varepsilon \leq \frac{1}{3}\}$. For all $\varepsilon \in E$, define our measure of divergence as $\Delta(\varepsilon) = 2\varepsilon$. Finally, define our measure of polarization to be $M := \min_{\varepsilon \in E} \Delta(\varepsilon) = 2c - b$. Clearly, M is increasing in c (and increasing in $-b$).

Higher Costs for Moderate Candidates

The analysis of changes in costs and benefits is remarkable in that it predicts increasing divergence even though candidates of all ideological stripes face the same nonideological costs and benefits. The argument for why increasing costs drives polarization thus does not depend on arguing that more-moderate candidates have a harder time running for office or find the legislature less profitable. Nevertheless, it is interesting to consider this addition to the model. What happens if moderates face higher costs (or, equivalently, lower benefits)?

The most immediate way to see what will happen is to focus on the most divergent equilibrium. The maximum amount of divergence possible is controlled by the fact that any more divergence will allow the median citizen to enter and gain enough votes to win the race. With fixed costs and benefits, it must be the case that the median citizen will prefer to do this. How do we know? Consider the entry decision of a median citizen in the case that she can win for sure, leaving b and c constant across ideology. If the median citizen sits out, her expected utility is

$$EU_m | NoRun = \frac{1}{2} - |x_m - (x_m - \varepsilon)| + \frac{1}{2} - |x_m - (x_m + \varepsilon)| = -\varepsilon.$$

On the other hand, if she enters, she wins for sure, so she receives

$$EU_m | Run = b - c.$$

Thus, to sustain a divergent two-candidate equilibrium in which the median citizen could run and win but chooses not to, we would need

$$b - c < -e,$$

or,

$$c - b > -e.$$

But we already saw before that to sustain a two-candidate equilibrium, we needed

$$c - \frac{b}{2} < \varepsilon$$

These two conditions cannot be simultaneously met. Thus, in any divergent two-candidate equilibrium, if the two candidates are so far apart that the median citizen can enter and win, he or she will choose to do so.

But what if the costs of running are decreasing in ideological extremity, so that the median citizen, as well as other relatively moderate citizens, face higher costs than those who are more extreme? The logic outlined in this appendix should make clear that now we can increase the most divergent equilibrium; whereas before this would induce the median citizen to enter and win, if now the median's costs are sufficiently high, the median citizen will choose to forgo running and tolerate the disutility of having an extremist on one side or the other represent him or her.

Estimating the Advantage of Moderates

In this appendix, I replicate the two main observational designs from existing research, but I extend them to include nonincumbents by using contribution-based scalings. I estimate the design from Canes-Wrone, Brady, and Cogan (2002) design using the equation

$$\text{(A2.1)} \quad DemVote_{it} = \beta_1\, DemExtemism_{it} + \beta_2\, RepExtremism_{it} + X_{it} + \varepsilon_{ijt},$$

where $DemVote_{it}$ is the Democratic share of the two-party vote in district i at time t (note that results are completely symmetrical if we use Republican vote share instead).

The explanatory variables of interest are $DemExtemism_{it}$ and $RepExtremism_{it}$, which are the absolute value of the Democratic and Republican candidates' CFScores, respectively. X_{it} stands in for a set of controls. This vector always includes the Democratic vote share in the most recent presidential election (available in the DIME data), year fixed effects, and the logged total amount of money raised by each candidate. In some specifications, I also add district fixed effects, so that we are looking at extremism and vote shares relative to overall district means.

I estimate the design of Ansolabehere, Snyder, and Stewart (2001), using the equation

$$\text{(A2.2)} \quad DemVote_{it} = \delta_1\, Midpoint_{it} + \delta_2\, Distance_{it} + X_{it} + \varepsilon_{ijt},$$

where $Midpoint_{it}$ is the midpoint (in this case, the average) of the two candidates' CFScores, and $Distance_{it}$ is the absolute value of the distance

TABLE A2.1 **The Advantage of Moderate Candidates, Contested U.S. House Races, 1980–2012, Using CFscores**

	Dem Vote Share			
Dem Extremism	−0.20	−0.11	...	...
	(0.02)	(0.03)	...	...
Rep Extremism	0.20	0.23	...	...
	(0.02)	(0.03)	...	...
Moderation (Midpoint)	...	...	0.30	0.27
	...	...	(0.02)	(0.04)
Distance Between Candidates	...	...	0.00	0.01
	...	...	(0.00)	(0.00)
Dem Pres Vote	0.52	0.50	0.53	0.50
	(0.02)	(0.03)	(0.02)	(0.03)
Log Dem Total Receipts	−0.04	−0.03	−0.04	−0.04
	(0.00)	(0.00)	(0.00)	(0.00)
Log Rep Total Receipts	0.04	0.04	0.04	0.04
	(0.00)	(0.00)	(0.00)	(0.00)
Observations	3,401	3,401	3,401	3,401
Year Fixed Effects	Yes	Yes	Yes	Yes
District Fixed Effects	No	Yes	No	Yes

Note: Robust standard errors in parentheses. Outcome variable is Democratic share of two-party vote. Dem Extremism, Rep Extremism, and Moderation are all scaled to run from 0 to 1 (min to max).

between the two candidates' CFScores. The control variables contained in X_{it} are the same as for the Canes-Wrone et. al. design. Note that, in all cases, I include only contested races, since this is necessary to compute the midpoint between the candidates.

Table A2.1 presents the results using CFScores. In all specifications and designs, we find large associations between ideological positions and vote share. Democratic vote share is predicted to (a) decrease when Democratic candidates take more-extreme positions; (b) increase when Republican candidates take more-extreme positions; and (c) increase when the midpoint between the two candidates shifts right while holding the distance between the candidates fixed, an indication that the Democratic candidate is more moderate.

A key challenge to these results is the possibility that the contribution-based scalings pick up donor expectations about electoral fortunes. Strategic donors may seek out candidates they think are going to become incumbents, regardless of party, which might make candidates who are expected to do well look more "moderate." This is why, in each regression, I control for the total amount of money raised. This means that we are making comparisons among candidates who have raised the same amount of money—

and are thus equally popular among donors—yet who offer ideological platforms.

To further probe the validity of these estimates, I now reestimate the same designs and specifications, but defining extremism based on DW-DIME scores rather than CFScores. As table A2.2 shows, we continue to find similar estimates. The results are not driven by the particularities of the CFscore scalings.

Next, I reestimate the results using Hall-Snyder scores. As table A2.3 shows, we again find a large advantage for moderate candidates. No matter what scaling we choose, we always find the same answer.

Finally, I reestimate all three tables focusing only on contested, open-seat races, where no incumbents are present, as shown in tables A2.4, A2.5, and A2.6. These estimates are more demanding because they rely on far fewer observations; as a result, the estimates become less precise. Nevertheless, we continue to see the same patterns. Democrats do worse when Democratic positions are more extreme and do better when Republican positions are more extreme, on average. This is true across the scalings (the Rep Extremism coefficient in the DW-DIME analysis does attenuate, as does one Dem Extremism coefficient in the Hall-Snyder analysis, but the majority of the estimates of interest remain large across the tables).

TABLE A2.2 **The Advantage of Moderate Candidates, Contested U.S. House Races, 1980–2012, Using DW-DIME Scores**

	Dem Vote Share			
Dem Extremism	−0.09	−0.08	. . .	. . .
	(0.01)	(0.02)	. . .	. . .
Rep Extremism	0.08	0.11	. . .	. . .
	(0.01)	(0.02)	. . .	. . .
Moderation (Midpoint)	. . .	. . .	0.18	0.20
	. . .	. . .	(0.02)	(0.02)
Distance Between Candidates	. . .	. . .	−0.02	−0.00
	. . .	. . .	(0.01)	(0.01)
Dem Pres Vote	0.59	0.53	0.59	0.53
	(0.03)	(0.04)	(0.03)	(0.04)
Log Dem Total Receipts	−0.04	−0.04	−0.04	−0.04
	(0.00)	(0.01)	(0.00)	(0.01)
Log Rep Total Receipts	0.04	0.04	0.04	0.04
	(0.00)	(0.00)	(0.00)	(0.00)
Observations	2,338	2,338	2,338	2,338
Year Fixed Effects	Yes	Yes	Yes	Yes
District Fixed Effects	No	Yes	No	Yes

Note: Robust standard errors in parentheses. Outcome variable is Democratic share of two-party vote. Dem Extremism, Rep Extremism, and Moderation are all scaled to run from 0 to 1 (min to max).

TABLE A2.3 **The Advantage of Moderate Candidates, Contested U.S. House Races, 1980–2012, Using Hall-Snyder Scores**

	Dem Vote Share			
Dem Extremism	−0.15	−0.12	. . .	. . .
	(0.01)	(0.02)	. . .	. . .
Rep Extremism	0.11	0.20	. . .	. . .
	(0.01)	(0.01)	. . .	. . .
Moderation (Midpoint)	. . .	. . .	0.24	0.20
	. . .	. . .	(0.01)	(0.02)
Distance Between Candidates	. . .	. . .	−0.06	−0.04
	. . .	. . .	(0.01)	(0.02)
Dem Pres Vote	0.58	0.59	0.59	0.60
	(0.02)	(0.04)	(0.02)	(0.04)
Log Dem Total Receipts	−0.02	−0.02	−0.02	−0.02
	(0.00)	(0.00)	(0.00)	(0.00)
Log Rep Total Receipts	0.02	0.02	0.02	0.02
	(0.00)	(0.00)	(0.00)	(0.00)
Observations	2,439	2,439	2,439	2,439
Year Fixed Effects	Yes	Yes	Yes	Yes
District Fixed Effects	No	Yes	No	Yes

Note: Robust standard errors in parentheses. Outcome variable is Democratic share of two-party vote. Dem Extremism, Rep Extremism, and Moderation are all scaled to run from 0 to 1 (min to max).

TABLE A2.4 **The Advantage of Moderate Candidates, Contested Open-Seat U.S. House Races, 1980–2012, Using CFscores**

	Dem Vote Share			
Dem Extremism	−0.22	−0.24	. . .	. . .
	(0.05)	(0.12)	. . .	. . .
Rep Extremism	0.12	0.18	. . .	. . .
	(0.05)	(0.16)	. . .	. . .
Moderation (Midpoint)	. . .	. . .	0.26	0.35
	. . .	. . .	(0.04)	(0.15)
Distance Between Candidates	. . .	. . .	−0.01	−0.01
	. . .	. . .	(0.01)	(0.02)
Dem Pres Vote	0.57	0.54	0.58	0.53
	(0.05)	(0.10)	(0.05)	(0.09)
Log Dem Total Receipts	−0.02	−0.02	−0.02	−0.02
	(0.01)	(0.01)	(0.01)	(0.01)
Log Rep Total Receipts	0.03	0.03	0.03	0.03
	(0.00)	(0.01)	(0.00)	(0.01)
Observations	511	511	511	511
Year Fixed Effects	Yes	Yes	Yes	Yes
District Fixed Effects	No	Yes	No	Yes

Note: Robust standard errors in parentheses. Outcome variable is Democratic share of two-party vote. Dem Extremism, Rep Extremism, and Moderation are all scaled to run from 0 to 1 (min to max).

TABLE A2.5 **The Advantage of Moderate Candidates, Contested Open-Seat U.S. House Races, 1980–2012, Using DW-DIME Scores**

	Dem Vote Share			
Dem Extremism	−0.10	−0.13	...	...
	(0.02)	(0.07)	...	...
Rep Extremism	0.01	0.04	...	...
	(0.02)	(0.05)	...	...
Moderation (Midpoint)	...	...	0.13	0.13
	...	...	(0.03)	(0.08)
Distance Between Candidates	...	...	−0.07	−0.02
	...	...	(0.02)	(0.05)
Dem Pres Vote	0.56	0.56	0.57	0.55
	(0.06)	(0.14)	(0.06)	(0.14)
Log Dem Total Receipts	−0.03	−0.02	−0.03	−0.02
	(0.01)	(0.02)	(0.01)	(0.02)
Log Rep Total Receipts	0.03	0.03	0.03	0.03
	(0.01)	(0.01)	(0.01)	(0.01)
Observations	412	412	412	412
Year Fixed Effects	Yes	Yes	Yes	Yes
District Fixed Effects	No	Yes	No	Yes

Note: Robust standard errors in parentheses. Outcome variable is Democratic share of two-party vote. Dem Extremism, Rep Extremism, and Moderation are all scaled to run from 0 to 1 (min to max).

TABLE A2.6 **The Advantage of Moderate Candidates, Contested Open-Seat U.S. House Races, 1980–2012, Using Hall-Snyder Scores**

	Dem Vote Share			
Dem Extremism	−0.07	−0.04	...	...
	(0.02)	(0.06)	...	...
Rep Extremism	0.06	0.09	...	...
	(0.02)	(0.05)	...	...
Moderation (Midpoint)	...	...	0.14	0.15
	...	...	(0.02)	(0.07)
Distance Between Candidates	...	...	−0.02	0.02
	...	...	(0.02)	(0.05)
Dem Pres Vote	0.52	0.56	0.52	0.56
	(0.04)	(0.10)	(0.04)	(0.10)
Log Dem Total Receipts	−0.02	−0.02	−0.02	−0.02
	(0.00)	(0.01)	(0.00)	(0.01)
Log Rep Total Receipts	0.02	0.01	0.02	0.01
	(0.00)	(0.00)	(0.00)	(0.00)
Observations	486	486	486	486
Year Fixed Effects	Yes	Yes	Yes	Yes
District Fixed Effects	No	Yes	No	Yes

Note: Robust standard errors in parentheses. Outcome variable is Democratic share of two-party vote. Dem Extremism, Rep Extremism, and Moderation are all scaled to run from 0 to 1 (min to max).

RD Estimates of the Effects of Extremist Nominations

This section is simply an update of the regression discontinuity (RD) first presented in my earlier work (Hall 2015). I estimate models of the form

(A2.3) $WinGeneral_{it} = \beta_0 + \beta_1\ ExtremistPrimaryWin_{it} + f(V_{it}) + \varepsilon_{it},$

where $ExtremistPrimaryWin_{it}$ is an indicator variable for the extremist winning the primary in district i at time t. Thus β_1 is the quantity of interest, the RD estimator for causal effects from the "as-if" random assignment of an extremist in the general election. The variable $WinGeneral_{it}$ is an indicator for whether the nominee in district i wins the general election at time t.

The term $f(V_{it})$ represents a flexible function of the running variable, the extremist candidate's vote-share winning margin—that is, the extremist candidate's share of the top two candidates' vote less 0.5, which determines treatment status. There are many choices of specification and bandwidth for estimating the RD. I present a variety of specifications, including the automated technique from Calonico, Cattaneo, and Titiunik (2014), hereafter CCT, which uses a local kernel combined with an optimal bandwidth procedure, as implemented in the rdrobust package in Stata.

Finally, to address the issue that some primary races are between ideologically distinct candidates while others or not, I restrict the sample to only the set of races where the ideological distance between the top two candidates is at or above the median distance between the top two candidates across all races in the sample. This is in keeping with the method from my earlier work (Hall 2015).

Table A2.7 presents the results, for both vote share and the probability of winning the general election. We estimate very large penalties for nominating extremists. The estimates range from a penalty of 6 to 11 percentage points on vote share, and from 17 to 32 percentage points on win probability. The CCT technique estimates penalties of 8 percentage points on vote share and 27 percentage points on win probability. These are massive penalties to extremist nominees.

The key identifying assumption for this RD to extract causal effects of nominating more-extreme candidates is that candidates close to the discontinuity cannot "sort" into winning or losing. A number of scholars have shown some evidence that this assumption is violated in U.S. House general-election races, where barely winning candidates appear to be

TABLE A2.7 **The Advantage of Moderate Candidates, U.S. House Races, 1980–2012, Using Hall-Snyder Scores.**

	Vote Share				Victory			
Extremist	−0.11	−0.06	−0.06	−0.08	−0.32	−0.20	−0.17	−0.27
Nominee	(0.04)	(0.02)	(0.02)	(0.03)	(0.14)	(0.07)	(0.08)	(0.11)
N	228	909	909	375	229	920	920	364
Polynomial	1	3	5	CCT	1	3	5	CCT
District Fixed Effects	0.10	–	–	0.09	0.10	–	–	0.08

Note: Robust standard errors clustered by district in parentheses in columns 1–3 and 4–7; standard errors in columns 4 and 8 come from rdrobust package and are clustered by district. The running variable is the extremist primary candidate's vote-share winning margin in the primary.

disproportionately likely to be incumbents, relative to barely losing candidates (Grimmer et al. 2012; Caughey and Sekhon 2011; Jason Snyder 2005). Elsewhere (Hall 2015; Hall and Thompson forthcoming) I test for the validity of the primary RD design and find no evidence of sorting. Because these other writings of mine use almost exactly the same sample of elections as this analysis, I do not repeat these exercises here—but to sum up, in brief, primaries in which the extremist barely won look no different from those in which the more moderate candidate barely won on a variety of pretreatment traits including, most important, their previous general-election vote shares for one party or the other.

I do not repeat this RD analysis using CFScores or DW-DIME because both could suffer from posttreatment bias. Winning the primary could affect the contributions a candidate raises, and therefore the candidate's scaling, as well as his or her vote share. This is why in my earlier work (Hall 2015) I use the Hall-Snyder scalings, which addresses this posttreatment issue. That being said, despite these issues, in my more recent work I do present RD results using these alternative scalings and find similar results (Hall and Thompson forthcoming).

Replicating the RD Using State Legislator Ideal Points

Separate from the RD's identifying assumption, we might worry that the results are somehow driven by the choice to scale candidates based on campaign contributions. As a reminder, I am already using a particularly conservative scaling method that considers only the contributions that candidates receive before they become incumbents.

TABLE A2.8 **The Advantage of Moderate Candidates, U.S. House Races, 1980–2012, Focusing on State Legislators with NP-Scores**

	Vote Share				Victory			
Extremist	−0.04	−0.00	−0.08	−0.14	−0.31	−0.12	−0.29	−0.54
Nominee	(0.14)	(0.06)	(0.07)	(0.07)	(0.41)	(0.16)	(0.19)	(0.22)
N	23	116	116	52	23	116	116	47
Polynomial	1	3	5	CCT	1	3	5	CCT
District Fixed Effects	0.10	–	–	0.14	0.10	–	–	0.12

Note: Robust standard errors clustered by district in parentheses in columns 1–3 and 4–7; standard errors in columns 4 and 8 come from rdrobust package and are clustered by district. The running variable is the extremist primary candidate's vote-share winning margin in the primary.

To further test the robustness of the design, I now replicate the previous analysis using the state legislative data, as I explained in chapter 3. The drawback to this approach is that there is not nearly as much data; there are not a lot of cases where two state legislators are engaged in a close primary election. Nevertheless, table A2.8 presents the results, in the same format as table A2.7. Although the estimates are more fragile because of the small sample sizes, we find generally large and negative estimates (there is only one exception, the third-order polynomial on vote share, though this specification does estimate a large win probability penalty). The CCT optimal bandwidth estimates are large, negative, and statistically significant at the .05 level. Even when we completely avoid using campaign contributions to scale candidates, we continue to see evidence for large penalties to extremist nominees in the general election.

APPENDIX 3

Effects of Office Benefits
on Polarization

To estimate the causal effects of changes in legislator salaries, I use ordinary least squares (OLS) to estimate difference-in-differences equations of the form

(A3.1) $PolarizationofCandidatePool_{it} = \beta Log(Salary + 1)_{it} + \gamma_i + \delta_t + \varepsilon_{it},$

where $PolarizationofCandidatePool_{it}$ is the CFscore-based measure of candidate-pool polarization in state i at time t, as described in chapter 5. The main explanatory variable is simply the logged legislator salary in state i at time t, with 1 added to allow the inclusion of New Mexico's $0 salary, and γ_i and δ_t stand in for state and year fixed effects, respectively. Because the treatment is fixed at the state level, all standard errors are clustered at the state level. To assess the key identifying assumption of parallel trends, I also reestimate this equation with the addition of state-specific linear time trends. To help in interpreting the results, I rescale the log salary variable to run from 0, in the smallest case (New Mexico), to 1, in the largest case (California).

Table A3.1 presents the results. The first column reflects the vanilla difference-in-differences, which estimates a substantial decrease in the polarization of the candidate pool. The overall standard deviation of the candidate polarization measure is .22; the within-state standard deviation is .11. Moving from the smallest salary to the largest is therefore estimated to decrease the polarization by the candidate pool by more than 1.5 overall standard deviations, and by more than 3 within-state standard deviations.

TABLE A3.1 **Higher Salaries Decrease Polarization of Candidate Pool, U.S. State Legislatures, 1990–2012**

	Candidate Polarization		
Log Salary	−0.345	−0.286	−0.348
	(0.134)	(0.135)	(0.150)
Log Salary, $t + 1$	...	...	0.001
	...	...	(0.034)
Log Salary, $t + 2$	...	...	−0.045
	...	...	(0.089)
N	444	443	342
Year Fixed Effects	Yes	Yes	Yes
State Fixed Effects	Yes	Yes	Yes
State Trends	No	Yes	No

Note: Robust standard errors clustered by state in parentheses.

TABLE A3.2 **Effect of Higher Salaries on Polarization of State Legislatures**

	Legislative Polarization		
Log Salary	−0.282	−0.530	−0.316
	(0.369)	(0.246)	(0.392)
Log Salary, $t + 1$	...	...	0.075
	...	...	(0.106)
Log Salary, $t + 2$	...	...	−0.138
	...	...	(0.204)
N	393	391	314
Year Fixed Effects	Yes	Yes	Yes
State Fixed Effects	Yes	Yes	Yes
State Trends	No	Yes	No

Note: Robust standard errors clustered by state in parentheses.

The next two columns relax and test the parallel trends assumption. In the second column, we see that the addition of the state-specific linear trends does not attenuate the estimate—in fact, it becomes more negative.

In the third column, I include two leads of the log salary variable. If there is significant pretrending, then the inclusion of these variables should remove the coefficient on the main quantity of interest; yet, as we see, this coefficient is almost unchanged. Accordingly, the parallel trends assumption seems plausible. Taken together, we see strong evidence that increasing salaries decrease the polarization of the candidate pool.

Table A3.2 reestimates the same regressions, but now with legislative polarization as the outcome variable. Specifically, the NP-Score dataset provides a measure of the estimated distance between the party's medians in each state legislature. For simplicity, I estimate results using the upper chamber's polarization (results are similar using lower house polarization or their average.) As I discussed in chapter 5, we see a corresponding decrease in legislative polarization when salaries increase. Although the estimated effect is somewhat imprecise in the first column, it becomes substantially larger and more precise in the second column when state trends are added. It is noisier, but still large in magnitude, in the third column when salary leads are included.

Again, these effects are substantial in magnitude. The overall standard deviation of the polarization measure is .49, which means that the most precise estimate in column 2 reflects just over a 1 standard deviation decrease in polarization. The within-state standard deviation is .17, corresponding to a 3+ standard deviation effect in column 2.

Scare-Off of Moderates

As I discussed in chapter 5, the simple raw comparison of candidate pools when there are or are not incumbents could be biased. I now address this issue using two more-complex empirical designs. In the first, I employ a difference-in-differences design, examining districts that switch the party of their incumbent and looking at the subsequent changes in the ideology of the party's candidate pool. This strategy allows for the inclusion of a large number of observations and is thus most precise from a statistical point of view.

Specifically, I estimate equations of the form

$$\textbf{(A3.2)} \quad AverageDemCandIdeology_{ip,t+1} = \beta_1 DemWin_{ipt} + \gamma_i + \delta_t + \varepsilon_{ip,t+1}$$

where γ_i and δ_t represent district and year fixed effects, respectively. I estimate this equation separately for Democrats and for Republicans (replacing the word "Dem" with "Rep" in each case in equation A3.2). The quantity of interest is β_1, which measures the effect of Democratic (or Republican) incumbency on the ideology of the subsequent candidate pool for the Democrats (or Republicans) in that district in the next election cycle.

To address concerns that the so-called parallel trends assumption of the difference-in-differences design is invalid, I also implement a general-election regression discontinuity (RD) design (D. Lee 2008). In this alternate approach I look at the subsequent Democratic candidate pool after

TABLE A3.3 **Effect of Party Incumbency on Ideological Composition of Party Candidate Pool in Next Election Cycle**

	Ideology of Candidate Pool, $t + 1$			
	Difference-in-Differences		Regression Discontinuity (RD)	
	Dem	Rep	Dem	Rep
Party Incumbency	0.17	−0.20	0.30	−0.14
	(0.03)	(0.03)	(0.03)	(0.03)
Intercept	−0.74	0.89	−0.85	0.95
N	4,272	3,939	4,272	3,939
District Fixed Effects	Yes	Yes	No	No
Year Fixed Effects	Yes	Yes	No	No
RD Specification	–	–	Cubic	Cubic

Note: Last two columns include cubic specification of forcing variable (party's vote-share winning margin). Robust standard errors in parentheses.

"coin-flip" races in which a district just barely receives a Democrat or Republican incumbent.

For the RD, I estimate equations of the form

(A3.3) $AverageCandIdeology_{ip,t+1} = \beta_1 PartyWin_{ipt} + f(V_{ipt}) + \varepsilon_{ip,t+1},$

where $f(V_{ipt})$ is a flexible function of the new forcing variable, now defined as the party's vote-share winning margin. The idea in this approach is to compare the Democratic (or Republican) candidate pool after a close election wherein the Democrats (or Republicans) barely secured incumbency to the same candidate pool after a close election where the Republicans (or Democrats) barely secured incumbency. The difference in the ideology of the candidate pool across these two cases represents the causal effect of party incumbency on the candidate pool's ideology.

Table A3.3 presents the results from both approaches. The first two columns show the difference-in-differences results for the two parties, respectively. In the first column we see that Democratic Party incumbency causes approximately a 0.17-point increase in the average candidate ideology in the subsequent primary. Since more-negative scores mean more liberal, this increase represents a shift in the *moderate* direction caused by incumbency. Thus, when the Democrats lose the seat, their subsequent candidate pool becomes more extreme. The second column, for the Republicans, reveals the same pattern. When the Republicans win the seat, the subsequent candidate pool's average ideology decreases by a similar amount, indicating a shift in the moderate direction. Thus, when the Republicans lose the seat, and a Democratic incumbent is in office, the subsequent Republican pool becomes more ideologically extreme.

The final two columns show the estimates from the general-election RD. They are similar to the difference-in-differences estimates. In both cases, we again see party incumbency causing the party's candidate pool to become more extreme, indicating a scare-off of moderate challengers.

State Legislators Running for the U.S. House

Early in chapter 6, I showed that state legislators are more likely to run for the U.S. House of Representatives when they can do so without giving up their current seat. Now, I confirm this relationship more formally. Specifically, I estimate equations of the form

(A4.1) $$RunForHouse_{it} = \beta_0 + \beta_1 GiveUpSeat_{it} + X_{it} + \varepsilon_{it},$$

where $RunForHouse_{it}$ is an indicator variable for whether state legislator i chooses to run for the U.S. House in the election at time t. The variable $GiveUpSeat_{it}$ is an indicator variable for whether state legislator i has to give up his or her seat in the state legislature to run for the House at time t. Finally, X_{it} stands in for a set of control variables.

The coefficient of interest, β_1, measures how much more or less likely state legislators are to run for the House if they do not have to give up their seat to do so—that is, if it is much less costly to run. Table A4.1 presents the estimated results.

In the first column, I run a simple pooled regression. In any given electoral cycle, state legislators choose to run for the U.S. House when they have to give up their seats 1.4 percent of the time, as the second row (constant) shows; however, as the first row shows, this probability increases by 1.1 percentage points, to 2.5 percent in total, when they do not have to give up their seats to run. State legislators are almost twice as likely to run for the House when they can do so without risking control of their current offices.

In the second column, I add year fixed effects to account for potential differences over time in the rate of opportunities to run for the House

TABLE A4.1 **State Legislators More Likely to Run for U.S. House When Costs are Lower**

	Run for House		
Seat Not Up for Reelection	0.011	0.011	0.019
	(0.005)	(0.005)	(0.010)
Constant (Seat Up for Reelection)	0.014	–	–
	(0.003)	...	...
N	3,676	3,676	3,676
Year Fixed Effects	No	Yes	Yes
Legislator Fixed Effects	No	No	Yes

Note: Robust standard errors clustered by state in parentheses.

and the choice to do so. Again we see the probability of running increase substantially. In the final column, I add legislator fixed effects to perform a difference-in-differences design that compares the within-legislator change in the decision to run for the House when state legislators can do so without giving up their current seat to changes in running rates for other state senators in other states who do not have the same opportunity at the same time. Again, we see a marked increase in their propensity to run for the House when the cost of doing so is lower.

In the next analysis in chapter 6, I then showed that the manner in which legislators responded to the risk of having to give up their seats varied with their ideology. In chapter 6, I illustrated this finding with a simple graph showing that more-extreme legislators were more likely to run regardless of ideology, while more-moderate legislators were more sensitive to this cost. More formally, I now estimate equations of the form

$$\textbf{(A4.2)} \quad \begin{aligned} RunForHouse_{it} &= \beta_0 + \beta_1 GiveUpSeat_{it} \\ &+ \beta_2 GiveUpSeat_{it} \times Extremism_{it} + \beta_3 Extremism_{it} + X_{it} + \varepsilon_{it}. \end{aligned}$$

The coefficient β_1 thus indicates how much more likely moderate legislators (those with Extremism = 0) are to run for the U.S. House when they do not have to give up their state senate seat, relative to when they do have to. Extremism is defined two different ways. First, I define it as

$$\textbf{(A4.3)} \quad Extremism_{ipst} = |\, NPScore_{it} - MedianNPScore_{pst} \,|.$$

That is, legislator i in party p in state s's extremism at time t is the absolute distance between the legislator's NP-Score and the median NP-Score in his or her state and party at time t. To explore the robustness of this

TABLE A4.2 **State Legislators More Likely to Run for U.S. House When Ideology is More Extreme**

	Run for House	
Seat Not Up	0.017	0.016
	(0.008)	(0.011)
Seat Not Up × Extremism	−0.015	−0.016
	(0.015)	(0.010)
N	3,676	3,365
Year Fixed Effects	Yes	Yes
Legislator Fixed Effects	Yes	Yes
Measure	NP-Score	CF-Score

Note: Robust standard errors clustered by legislator in parentheses.
Main effect for extremism is absorbed by legislator fixed effects.

measure, I also define it analogously using CFScores. Both measures are standardized to have mean 0 and standard deviation 1.

The coefficient β_2, the main quantity of interest, reflects how much less or more sensitive legislators with more-extreme roll-call voting records are to the cost of giving up their seat to run for the House. A negative estimate for β_2 would thus indicate that more-extreme legislators are less sensitive to the costs of running for office.

Table A4.2 presents the estimated results, using NP-Score in the first column. In the first row of the first column, we see that, for a state senator with average extremism, there is a significant 1.7 percentage-point increase in the probability of running for the House when it is without cost to do so. As the second row shows, however, for a state senator who is one standard deviation more extreme than the average, this increase is only 0.2 percentage points. That is, for more-extreme state senators, the chance to run without cost has almost no effect on the probability of running for the House. As I stressed in chapter 6, this estimate is unfortunately not very precise.

In the second column, we redo the analysis with CFScores, finding similar patterns. Again, the effect is nearly 0 for state senators one standard deviation more extreme than the average. Here, the estimated difference in the effect is a bit more precise.

Notes

Introduction

Epigraph sources: Franklin 1987; Gupta 2013.

1. Note that Larson is a longtime member of Congress, not one of the first-year members there to view the presentation.

2. These outlets are RealClearPolitics, the Atlantic, the National Journal, and MSNBC. Found via Google search for the phrase "Why Would Anyone Run For Congress," February 3, 2015.

Chapter One

Epigraph sources: Key 1966, 6–7; Adams 1980, 197.

1. Fiorina, Abrams, and Pope (2008) raise this point in their discussion of the literature: "When statistical relationships change, students of voting behavior have a tendency to locate the source of the change in voter attitudes, but unchanging voters may simply be responding to changes in candidate strategy and behavior" (556).

2. The midpoint of the scale, at 0, is actually arbitrary, but it is a rough proxy for "moderate." Essentially all Democrats are to the left of 0, and essentially all Republicans are to the right of 0, so selecting candidates closest to 0 almost always means choosing the rightmost Democrat or the leftmost Republican.

3. For more information on data collection through the Database on Ideology, Money in Politics, Elections (DIME), see Bonica 2016. The DW added to DIME stands for "dynamic, weighted" and is a reference to the DW-NOMINATE methodology I will discuss later.

4. Fowler and Hall (2015) push this evidence further, exploring not overall ideological divergence but instead issue-specific divergence. Even if candidates fail to converge in general, the increased salience of particular issues might lead them to converge at least partially in some cases. Surprisingly, Fowler and Hall find no

evidence that this prediction holds. Divergence remains just as large even in cases where districts care a great deal about a particular issue.

Chapter Two

Epigraph sources: Tweedledee5 2014; Williams 2010. These quotations also appear in the epigraph to Hall and Thompson forthcoming.

1. A related literature uses surveys to look at the link between candidate ideology and reported vote choice. Stone and Simas (2010, abstract), for example, use voter positions from the 2006 national Cooperative Congressional Election Study (CCES) combined with expert evaluations of candidate positions and argue that "challengers can reap electoral rewards by taking more extreme positions relative to their districts." Studying the same 2006 survey and using the same expert evaluations, Joesten and Stone (2014, abstract) conclude instead that "proximity voting is common"—that is, they find that candidates whose ideological positions are closer to the self-reported positions of voters do better, electorally.

2. NOMINATE is an acronym for Nominal Three-Step Estimation, a scaling methodology developed by Poole and Rosenthal (1985). The more recent DW variant stands for "dynamic, weighted." For an accessible overview of the NOMINATE technique for nonstatisticians, see Emerson, Wiseman, and Vallely n.d.

3. Personal correspondence with Adam Bonica, May 21, 2016.

4. In some cases, we may be interested in ideology as represented by roll-call vote behavior on high-stakes votes or for some other set of votes (Clinton 2006).

5. The text for this paragraph comes from Hall and Thompson forthcoming.

6. Survey evidence also suggests that this may be the case, though the typical difficulties with scaling voters based on surveys always apply. Bafumi and Herron (2010), for example, jointly scale voters and candidates and conclude that American politics features exactly this kind of "leapfrog" democracy in which representation alternates between Democratic and Republican candidates to either side of the median voter.

Chapter Three

1. For the few cases of runoff primaries, I include the candidates and vote shares of the two-candidate runoff election.

Chapter Four

Epigraph sources: Schlesinger 1966; O'Donnell 2016.

1. 144 Cong. Rec. 14,231 (daily ed. June 25, 1998) (statement of Lee H. Hamilton). https://books.google.com/books?id=o6b2i2k5MkQC&pg=PA14231&lpg=PA14

231&dq=%22Candidates+today+ara+engaged+in+an+ever-escalating+effort
+to+raise+money%22&source=bl&ots=eoIf18HG7H&sig=g9XbdeUdir74Mqgey
m4LfSqCoqc&hl=en&sa=X&ved=0ahUKEwjHgb-35pDbAhVB9WMKHUf9DXI
Q6AEIKTAA#v=onepage&q=%22Candidates%20today%20are%20engaged%20
in%20an%20ever-escalating%20effort%20to%20raise%20money%22&f=false.
Emphasis mine.

2. *A Look at H.R. 1826, and the Public Financing of Congressional Campaigns: Hearing before the Committee on House Administration*, 111th Cong. (2009), http:// www.gpo.gov/fdsys/pkg/CHRG-111hhrg52711/html/CHRG-111hhrg52711.htm. Emphasis mine.

3. The reasons for this decrease in real pay are beyond the scope of this study, but we can speculate. Congressional salaries are nominally set to adjust annually based on wages to other fields, but members of Congress often seem to be pressured to reject these increases. This pressure seems to have increased over time — indeed, in 2012, Congress passed legislation freezing congressional salaries. For more information on the process, see Brudnick 2014.

Chapter Five

1. *Alaska State Officers Compensation Commission Findings and Recommendations*, January 10, 2009. http://doa.alaska.gov/dop/fileadmin/socc/pdf/bkgrnd_socc24 .pdf.

2. *Alaska State Officers Compensation Commission Findings*.

3. There was some subsequent discussion of cutting back Alaskan legislator salaries. However, as of early 2018, no pay cut had yet occurred (Herz 2018).

4. Michigan also implemented a large salary increase during the study period; however, it does not appear to be feasible to find a good synthetic match for Michigan in the data.

Chapter Six

1. Keen observers of politics may recall that Rand Paul, a U.S. senator from Kentucky, successfully circumvented this rule while attempting to run for both president and the Senate in 2016.

2. This number (28 percent) is calculated using the primary- and general-election data set from Hirano et al. (2010), which builds off Gary Jacobson's (1989) data set on previous officeholder experience. Using these data, I simply calculate the proportion of all candidates and all races who are listed as having held either a state senate or state house seat at any time in the past. Candidates who run for office more than once (including incumbents) are thus counted once each time they run.

Conclusion

Epigraph source: Key 1966.

1. This quotation is from his speech "Dangers of a Salaried Bureaucracy" (Franklin 1787).

Appendix One

1. Here I am glossing over a few extra technicalities. One is that we must also establish that there aren't other candidates who'd like to run, even if they would lose, simply to alter the identity of the winner. This possibility can be ruled out for the two-candidate case easily, as shown in Osborne and Slivinski 1996.

References

Abadie, Alberto, Alexis Diamond, and Jens Hainmueller. 2010. "Synthetic Control Methods for Comparative Case Studies: Estimating the Effect of California's Tobacco Control Program." *Journal of the American Statistical Association* 105 (490): 493–505.

Abramowitz, Alan I. 2011. *The Disappearing Center: Engaged Citizens, Polarization, and American Democracy*. New Haven, CT: Yale University Press.

Achen, Christopher H., and Larry M. Bartels. 2016a. *Democracy for Realists: Why Elections Do Not Produce Responsive Government*. Princeton, NJ: Princeton University Press.

———. 2016b. "Opinion: Do Sanders Supporters Favor His Policies?" *New York Times*, May 23, 2016. https://www.nytimes.com/2016/05/23/opinion/campaign-stops/do-sanders-supporters-favor-his-policies.html.

Adams, Douglas. 1980. *The Restaurant at the End of the Universe*. New York: Del Rey Books.

Ahler, Douglas J., and David E. Broockman. 2016. "The Delegate Paradox: Why Polarized Politicians Can Represent Citizens Best." Working paper, Stanford Graduate School of Business.

Aldrich, John H. 1995. *Why Parties? The Origin and Transformation of Political Parties in America*. Chicago: University of Chicago Press.

Aldrich, John H., and David W. Rohde. 2001. "The Logic of Conditional Party Government: Revisiting the Electoral Connection." In *Congress Reconsidered*, 7th ed., ed. Lawrence Dodd and Bruce Oppenheimer, 269–92. Thousand Oaks, CA: CQ Press.

Aldrich, J[ohn]. H., D. W. Rohde, and M. W. Tofias. 2007. "One D Is Not Enough: Measuring Conditional Party Government, 1887–2002." In *Party, Process, and Policy Making: Further New Perspectives on the History of Congress*, ed. David Brady and Mathew D. McCubbins, 102–13. Stanford, CA: Stanford University Press.

Alesina, Alberto. 1988. "Credibility and Policy Convergence in a Two-Party System with Rational Voters." *American Economic Review* 78 (4): 796–805.

Alt, James, Ethan Bueno de Mesquita, and Shanna Rose. 2011. "Disentangling Accountability and Competence in Elections: Evidence from U.S. Term Limits." *Journal of Politics* 73 (1): 171–86.

A Member of Congress [pseud.]. 2015. "Confessions of a Congressman: Nine Secrets from the Inside." Vox. Last updated July 12, 2015. https://www.vox.com/2015/2/5/7978823/congress-secrets.

Ansolabehere, Stephen, John M. de Figueiredo, and James M. Snyder. 2003. "Why Is There So Little Money in US Politics?" *Journal of Economic Perspectives* 17 (1): 105–30.

Ansolabehere, Stephen, John Mark Hansen, Shigeo Hirano, and James M. Snyder Jr. 2010. "More Democracy: The Direct Primary and Competition in US Elections." *Studies in American Political Development* 24 (2): 190–205.

Ansolabehere, Stephen, and Philip Edward Jones. 2010. "Constituents' Responses to Congressional Roll-Call Voting." *American Journal of Political Science* 54 (3): 583–97.

Ansolabehere, Stephen, James M. Snyder Jr., and Charles Stewart III. 2001. "Candidate Positioning in U.S. House Elections." *American Journal of Political Science* 45 (1): 136–59.

APSA Committee Report. 1950. "Toward a More Responsible Two-Party System." Supplement, *American Political Science Review* 44, no. 3 (September), pt. 2.

Aranson, Peter H., and Peter C. Ordeshook. 1972. "Spatial Strategy for Sequential Elections." In *Probability Models of Collective Decision Making*, ed. Richard G. Niemi and Herbert F. Weisberg. Columbus, OH: Charles E. Merrill.

Bafumi, Joseph, and Michael C. Herron. 2010. "Leapfrog Representation and Extremism: A Study of American Voters and Their Members in Congress." *American Political Science Review* 104 (3): 519–542.

Bai, Matt. 2014. *All the Truth Is Out: The Week Politics Went Tabloid*. New York, NY: Alfred A. Knopf.

Barber, Michael J. 2015. "Ideological Donors, Contribution Limits, and the Polarization of American Legislatures." *Journal of Politics* 78 (1): 296–310.

Barber, Michael J., Brandice Canes-Wrone, and Sharece Thrower. 2017. "Sophisticated Donors: Which Candidates Do Individual Contributors Finance?" *American Journal of Political Science* 61 (2): 271–88.

Baum, Matthew A. 2002. "Sex, Lies, and War: How Soft News Brings Foreign Policy to the Inattentive Public." *American Political Science Review* 96 (1): 91–109.

Besley, Timothy. 2004. "Paying Politicians: Theory and Evidence." *Journal of the European Economic Association* 2:193–215.

———. 2006. *Principled Agents? The Political Economy of Good Government*. Oxford: Oxford University Press.

Besley, Timothy, and Anne Case. 1995. "Does Electoral Accountability Affect Economic Policy Choices? Evidence From Gubernatorial Term Limits." *Quarterly Journal of Economics* 110 (3): 769–98.

Besley, Timothy, and Stephen Coate. 1997. "An Economic Model of Representative Democracy." *Quarterly Journal of Economics* 112 (1): 85–114.

Besley, Timothy, Olle Folke, Torsten Persson, and Johanna Rickne. 2017. "Gender Quotas and the Crisis of the Mediocre Man: Theory and Evidence from Sweden." *American Economic Review* 107 (8): 2204–42.

Besley, Timothy, and Marta Reynal-Querol. 2011. "Do Democracies Select More Educated Leaders?" *American Political Science Review* 105 (3): 552–66.

Bonica, Adam. 2013. "Ideology and Interests in the Political Marketplace." *American Journal of Political Science* 57 (2): 294–311.

———. 2014. "Mapping the Ideological Marketplace." *American Journal of Political Science* 58 (2): 367–86.

———. 2016. Database on Ideology, Money in Politics, and Elections: Public version 2.0 [computer file], March 16, 2016. Stanford, CA: Stanford University Libraries. https://data.stanford.edu /dime.

———. 2017. "Are Voters to Blame for Congressional Polarization?" Working paper.

———. Forthcoming. "Inferring Roll Call Scores from Campaign Contributions Using Supervised Machine Learning." *American Journal of Political Science.*

Brady, David W., Hahrie Han, and Jeremy C. Pope. 2007. "Primary Elections and Candidate Ideology: Out of Step with the Primary Electorate?" *Legislative Studies Quarterly* 32 (1): 79–105.

Brammer, Jack. 2016. "Some Businesses Could Reject Gay Clients under Bill Approved by Kentucky Senate." *Kansas City Star*, March 15, 2016. http://www.kansascity.com/news/politics-government/article66270867.html.

Brudnick, Ida A. 2014. "Salaries of Members of Congress: Recent Actions and Historical Tables." *Congressional Research Service Report* 7–5700.

Burden, Barry C. 2001. "The Polarizing Effects of Congressional Primaries." In *Congressional Primaries and Political Representation*, ed. Peter F. Galderisi, Marni Ezra, and Michael Lyons, 95–115. Lanham, MD: Rowman and Littlefield.

———. 2004. "Candidate Positioning in US Congressional Elections." *British Journal of Political Science* 34 (2): 211–27.

Calonico, Sebastian, Mattias D. Cattaneo, and Rocío Titiunik. 2014. "Robust Nonparametric Confidence Intervals for Regression-Discontinuity Designs." *Econometrica* 82 (6): 2295–2326.

Campbell, Angus, Philip E. Converse, Warren E. Miller, and Donald E. Stokes. 1960. *The American Voter*. Chicago: University of Chicago Press.

Canes-Wrone, Brandice, David W. Brady, and John F. Cogan. 2002. "Out of Step, Out of Office: Electoral Accountability and House Members' Voting." *American Political Science Review* 96 (1): 127–40.

Carson, Jamie L., Michael H. Crespin, Charles J. Finocchiaro, and David W. Rohde. 2007. "Redistricting and Party Polarization in the U.S. House of Representatives." *American Politics Research* 35 (6): 878–904.

Caughey, Devin M., and Jasjeet S. Sekhon. 2011. "Elections and the Regression Discontinuity Design: Lessons from Close U.S. House Races, 1942–2008." *Political Analysis* 19 (4): 385–408.

Clinton, Joshua D. 2006. "Representation in Congress: Constituents and Roll Calls in the 106th House." *Journal of Politics* 68 (2): 397–409.

Cohen, M., D. Karol, H. Noel, and J. Zaller. 2008. *The Party Decides: Presidential Nominations before and after Reform*. Chicago: University of Chicago Press.

Coleman, James S. 1971. "Internal Processes Governing Party Positions in Elections." *Public Choice* 11:35–60.

Condon, Stephanie. 2012. "Why Is Congress a Millionaires' Club?" CBS News, March 27, 2012. http://www.cbsnews.com/news/why-is-congress-a-millionaires -club/.

Converse, Philip. 1964. "The Nature of Belief Systems in Mass Publics." In *Ideology and Discontent*, ed. David E. Apter. New York: Free Press.

Council of State Governments. 2018. "Book of the States." Accessed May 31, 2018. http://knowledgecenter.csg.org/kc/category/content-type/content-type/book -states.

Cox, Gary W., and Jonathan N. Katz. 1996. "Why Did the Incumbency Advantage in U.S. House Elections Grow?" *American Journal of Political Science* 40 (2): 478–97.

Cox, Gary W., and Mathew D. McCubbins. 2005. *Setting the Agenda: Responsible Party Government in the U.S. House of Representatives*. New York: Cambridge University Press.

———. 2007. *Legislative Leviathan: Party Government in the House*. 2nd ed. New York: Cambridge University Press.

Dal Bó, Ernesto, Frederico Finan, Olle Folke, Torsten Persson, and Johanna Rickne. 2017. "Who Becomes a Politician?" *Quarterly Journal of Economics* 132 (4): 1877–1914.

Dal Bó, Ernesto, Frederico Finan, and Martín A. Rossi. 2013. "Strengthening State Capabilities: The Role of Financial Incentives in the Call to Public Service." *Quarterly Journal of Economics* 128 (3): 1169–1218.

Downs, Anthony. 1957. *An Economic Theory of Democracy*. New York: Harper and Row.

Drutman, Lee, and Alexander Furnas. 2014. "K Street Pays Top Dollar for Revolving Door Talent." Sunlight Foundation. January 21, 2014. https://sunlightfoun dation.com/2014/01/21/revolving-door-lobbyists-government-experience/.

Eggers, Andrew, Anthony Fowler, Jens Hainmueller, Andrew B. Hall, and James M. Snyder Jr. 2015. "On the Validity of the Regression Discontinuity Design for Estimating Electoral Effects: Evidence from over 40,000 Close Races." *American Journal of Political Science* 59 (1): 259–74.

Eggers, Andrew C., and Jens Hainmueller. 2009. "MPs for Sale? Returns to Office in Postwar British Politics." *American Political Science Review* 103 (4): 513.

Eilperin, Juliet. 2007. *Fight Club Politics: How Partisanship Is Poisoning the House of Representatives*. Lanham, MD: Rowman and Littlefield.

Emerson, Phil, Jim Wiseman, and Rick Vallely. n.d. *NOMINATE and American Political History: A Primer*. Accessed April 25, 2018. http://www.swarthmore.edu /SocSci/rvalell1/documents/Nominate_000.pdf.

Erikson, Robert S. 1971. "The Electoral Impact of Congressional Roll Call Voting." *American Political Science Review* 65 (4): 1018–32.

Erikson, Robert S., and Gerald C. Wright. 2000. "Representation of Constituency Ideology in Congress." In *Continuity and Change in House Elections*, ed. David W. Brady, John F. Cogan, and Morris P. Fiorina. Stanford, CA: Stanford University Press.

Fearon, James D. 1999. "Electoral Accountability and the Control of Politicians: Selecting Good Types versus Sanctioning Poor Performance." In *Democracy, Accountability, and Representation*, ed. Bernard Mann, Adam Przeworski, and Susan C. Stokes, 55–97. Cambridge: Cambridge University Press.

Feigenbaum, James J., Alexander Fouirnaies, and Andrew B. Hall. 2017. "The Majority Party Disadvantage: Revising Theories of Legislative Organization." *Quarterly Journal of Political Science* 12 (3): 269–300.

Fiorina, Morris P. 1994. "Divided Government in the American States: A Byproduct of Legislative Professionalism?" *American Political Science Review* 88 (2): 304–16.

Fiorina, Morris P., and Samuel J. Abrams. 2009. *Disconnect: The Breakdown of Representation in American Politics*. Norman: University of Oklahoma Press.

Fiorina, Morris P., Samuel J. Abrams, and Jeremy C. Pope. 2005. *Culture War? The Myth of a Polarized America*. New York: Pearson Longman.

———. 2008. "Polarization in the American Public: Misconceptions and Misreadings." *Journal of Politics* 70 (4): 556–60.

Fouirnaies, Alexander. 2016. "What Are the Electoral Consequences of Campaign Spending Limits?" Working paper, University of Chicago.

Fouirnaies, Alexander, and Andrew B. Hall. 2014. "The Financial Incumbency Advantage: Causes and Consequences." *Journal of Politics* 76 (3): 711–24.

———. 2018. "How Do Interest Groups Seek Access to Committees?" *American Journal of Political Science* 62 (1): 132–47.

Fowler, Anthony. 2018. "Partisan Intoxication or Policy Voting?" Working paper, University of Chicago, March. https://drive.google.com/file/d/1QxDrA_vzO-x _FxPmVQ1lLnPdFS3XmG7a/view.

Fowler, Anthony, and Andrew B. Hall. 2016. "The Elusive Quest for Convergence." *Quarterly Journal of Political Science* 11(1): 131–149.

———. 2017. "Long Term Consequences of Election Results." British Journal of Political Science 47 (2): 351–72.

Fowler, Linda L. 1993. *Candidates, Congress, and the American Democracy*. Ann Arbor: University of Michigan Press.

Franklin, Benjamin. 1787. "Dangers of a Salaried Bureaucracy." Bartelby.com. Accessed May 31, 2018. http://www.bartleby.com/268/8/12.html.

Gagliarducci, Stefano, and Tommaso Nannicini. 2013. "Do Better Paid Politicians Perform Better? Disentangling Incentives from Selection." *Journal of the European Economic Association* 11 (2): 369–98.

Gerber, Alan, Andrew Gooch, and Greg Huber. 2017. "Evaluations of Candidates' Non-Policy Characteristics from Issue Positions: Evidence about Valence Spillover." Working paper, Yale University.

Gilligan, Thomas W., and Keith Krehbiel. 1987. "Collective Decisionmaking and Standing Committees: An Informational Rationale for Restrictive Amendment Procedures." *Journal of Law, Economics and Organization* 3 (2): 287–335.

Glass, Ira, host. 2012. "Take the Money and Run for Office." *This American Life.* March 30. Program produced in collaboration with WBEZ Chicago and delivered to stations by PRX the Public Radio Exchange. http://www.thisamericanlife .org/radio-archives/episode/461/transcript.

Grim, Ryan, and Sabrina Siddiqui. 2017. "Call Time for Congress Shows How Fundraising Dominates Bleak Work Life." *HuffPost.* Last updated December 6, 2017. http://www.huffingtonpost.com/2013/01/08/call-time-congressional -fundraising_n_2427291.html.

Grimmer, Justin, Eitan Hersh, Brian Feinstein, and Daniel Carpenter. 2012. "Are Close Elections Random?" Paper presented at the 2012 Annual Meeting of the Midwest Political Science Association, Chicago, April 12–15.

Grimmer, Justin, and Eleanor Neff Powell. 2016. "Money in Exile: Campaign Contributions and Committee Access." *Journal of Politics* 78 (4): 974–88.

Gupta, Prachi. 2013. "Must-See Morning Clip: Asif Mandvi Hunts for a New Congressional Candidate." *Salon*, July 26, 2013. https://www.salon.com/2013/07/26 /must_see_morning_clip_aasif_mandvi_hunts_for_a_new_congressional_candidate/.

Hall, Andrew B. 2014. "How the Public Funding of Elections Increases Candidate Polarization." Working paper, Department of Government, Harvard University, August 13. http://www.andrewbenjaminhall.com/Hall_publicfunding.pdf.

———. 2015. "What Happens When Extremists Win Primaries?" *American Political Science Review* 109 (1): 18–42.

Hall, Andrew B., and Kenneth A. Shepsle. 2014. "The Changing Value of Seniority in the U.S. House: Conditional Party Government Revised." *Journal of Politics* 76 (1): 98–114.

Hall, Andrew B., and James M. Snyder Jr. 2015a. "Candidate Ideology and Electoral Success." Working paper, Department of Political Science, Stanford University, September 29. http://www.andrewbenjaminhall.com/Hall_Snyder_Ide ology.pdf.

———. 2015b. "How Much of the Incumbency Advantage Is Due to Scare-off?" *Political Science Research and Methods* 3 (3): 493–514.

Hall, Andrew B., and Daniel M. Thompson. Forthcoming. "Who Punishes Extremist Nominees? Candidate Ideology and Turning Out the Base in U.S. Elections."

American Political Science Review. Cambridge FirstView, March 7, 2018. https://doi.org/10.1017/S0003055418000023.

Harbridge, Laurel, and Neil Malhotra. 2011. "Electoral Incentives and Partisan Conflict in Congress: Evidence from Survey Experiments." *American Journal of Political Science* 55 (3): 494–510.

Hasbrouck, Paul D. 1927. *Party Government in the House of Representatives*. New York: Macmillan.

Herz, Nathaniel. 2018. "Commission Backtracks, Says No Pay Cut for Alaska Legislators." *Anchorage Daily News*, January 9, 2018. https://www.adn.com/pol itics/alaska-legislature/2018/01/09/commission-backtracks-says-no-to-pay-cut -for-alaska-legislators/.

Hill, Seth J., and Gregory A. Huber. 2017. "Representativeness and Motivations of the Contemporary Donorate: Results from Merged Survey and Administrative Records." *Political Behavior* 39 (1) 3–29.

Hill, Seth J., and Chris Tausanovitch. 2017. "Southern Realignment, Party Sort- ing, and the Polarization of American Primary Electorates, 1958–2012." *Public Choice*. Published ahead of print, October 16. https://link.springer.com/article /10.1007%2Fs11127-017-0478-0.

Hirano, Shigeo, James M. Snyder Jr., Stephen Ansolabehere, and John Mark Han- sen. 2010. "Primary Elections and Partisan Polarization in the US Congress." *Quarterly Journal of Political Science* 5 (2): 169–91.

Jacobson, Gary C. 1989. "Strategic Politicians and the Dynamics of U.S. House Elections, 1946–86." *American Political Science Review* 83 (3): 773–93.

———. 2012. *The Politics of Congressional Elections*. Upper Saddle River, NJ: Pear- son Education.

Jenkins, Jeffery A., and Charles Stewart III. 2012. *Fighting for the Speakership: The House and the Rise of Party Government*. Princeton, NJ: Princeton University Press.

Joesten, Danielle A., and Walter J. Stone. 2014. "Reassessing Proximity Voting: Expertise, Party, and Choice in Congressional Elections." *Journal of Politics* 76 (3): 740–53.

Kanthak, Kristin, and Jonathan Woon. 2015. "Women Don't Run? Election Aver- sion and Candidate Entry." *American Journal of Political Science* 59 (3): 595–612.

Key, Valdimer Orlando. 1965. *American State Politics: An Introduction*. New York: Alfred Knopf.

———. 1966. *The Responsible Electorate*. Cambridge, MA: Belknap Press of Har- vard University Press.

Kinder, Donald R., and Nathan P. Kalmoe. 2017. *Neither Liberal nor Conservative: Ideological Innocence in the American Public*. Chicago: University of Chicago Press.

Klein, Ezra. "For Elites, Politics Is Driven by Ideology; for Voters, It's Not." Vox. November 9, 2017. https://www.vox.com/policy-and-politics/2017/11/9/16614672 /ideology-liberal-conservatives.

Krehbiel, Keith. 1990. "Are Congressional Committees Composed of Preference Outliers?" *American Political Science Review* 84 (1): 149–63.

———. 1998. *Pivotal Politics: A Theory of U.S. Lawmaking*. Chicago: University of Chicago Press.

Lawless, Jennifer L., and Richard L. Fox. 2005. *It Takes a Candidate: Why Women Don't Run for Office*. New York: Cambridge University Press.

———. 2015. *Running from Office: Why Young Americans are Turned Off to Politics*. New York: Oxford University Press.

Lee, David S. 2008. "Randomized Experiments from Non-Random Selection in U.S. House Elections." *Journal of Econometrics* 142 (2): 675–97.

Lee, David S., Enrico Moretti, and Matthew J. Butler. 2004. "Do Voters Affect or Elect Policies? Evidence from the U.S. House." *Quarterly Journal of Economics* 119 (3): 807–59.

Lee, Frances. 2009. *Beyond Ideology: Politics, Principles, and Partisanship in the U.S. Senate*. Chicago: University of Chicago Press.

Lenz, Gabriel S. 2012. *Follow the Leader? How Voters Respond to Politicians' Performance and Policies*. Chicago: University of Chicago Press.

Levitz, Eric. 2017. "Democrats Can Abandon the Center—Because the Center Doesn't Exist." *New York*, July 30, 2017. http://nymag.com/daily/intelligencer/2017/07/dems-can-abandon-the-center-because-the-center-doesnt-exist.html.

Lewis, Jeffrey B., Keith Poole, Howard Rosenthal, Adam Boche, Aaron Rudkin, and Luke Sonnet. 2017. Voteview: Congressional Roll-Call Votes Database. https://voteview.com/.

Londregan, John, and James M. Snyder Jr. 1994. "Comparing Committee and Floor Preferences." *Legislative Studies Quarterly* 19 (2): 233–66.

Los Angeles Times. 1987. "Hart Statement Text: 'I'm Not a Beaten Man; I'm an Angry, Defiant Man.'" May 9, 1987. http://articles.latimes.com/1987-05-09/news/mn-4818_1_proud-man/2.

Maestas, Cherie D., Sarah Fulton, L. Sandy Maisel, and Walter J. Stone. 2006. "When to Risk It? Institutions, Ambitions, and the Decision to Run for the U.S. House." *American Political Science Review* 100 (5): 195–208.

Magleby, David B., and Candice J. Nelson. 2010. *The Money Chase: Congressional Campaign Finance Reform*. Washington, DC: Brookings Institution Press.

Maisel, Sandy, and Walter J. Stone. 2014. "Candidate Emergence Revisited: The Lingering Effects of Recruitment, Ambition, and Successful Prospects among House Candidates." *Political Science Quarterly* 129 (3): 429–47.

Masket, Seth E., Jonathan Winburn, and Gerald C. Wright. 2012. "The Gerrymanderers Are Coming! Legislative Redistricting Won't Affect Competition or Polarization Much, No Matter Who Does It." *PS: Political Science and Politics* 45 (1): 39–43.

Mayhew, David R. 1974. *Congress: The Electoral Connection*. Vol. 26. New Haven, CT: Yale University Press.

McCarty, Nolan. 2014. "The Decline of Regular Order in Appropriations: Does It Matter?" Working paper, Princeton University, December 12. https://www .princeton.edu/~nmccarty/appropriations.pdf.

McCarty, Nolan M., Keith T. Poole, and Howard Rosenthal. 2006. *Polarized America: The Dance of Ideology and Unequal Riches*. Cambridge, MA: MIT Press.

———. 2009. "Does Gerrymandering Cause Polarization?" *American Journal of Political Science* 53 (3): 666–80.

McGhee, Eric, Seth Masket, Boris Shor, Steven Rogers, and Nolan McCarty. 2014. "A Primary Cause of Partisanship? Nomination Systems and Legislator Ideology." *American Journal of Political Science* 58 (2): 337–51.

Miller, Warren E., and Donald E. Stokes. 1963. "Constituency Influence in Congress." *American Political Science Review* 57 (1): 45–56.

Noel, Hans. 2014. *Political Ideologies and Political Parties in America*. New York: Cambridge University Press.

O'Donnell, Norah. 2016. "Are Members of Congress Becoming Telemarketers?" CBS News, April 24, 2016. https://www.cbsnews.com/news/60-minutes-are-mem bers-of-congress-becoming-telemarketers/.

O'Keefe, Ed. 2013. "Tom Harkin: It's Somebody Else's Turn.'" *Washington Post*, January 26, 2013. https://www.washingtonpost.com/news/post-politics/wp/2013 /01/26/tom-harkin-its-somebody-elses-turn/?utm_term=.5cab7a22f0e5.

Osborne, Martin J. 2004. *An Introduction to Game Theory*. Oxford: Oxford University Press.

Osborne, Martin J., and Al Slivinski. 1996. "A Model of Political Competition with Citizen-Candidates." *Quarterly Journal of Economics* 111 (1): 65–96.

Owen, Guillermo, and Bernard Grofman. 2006. "Two-Stage Electoral Competition in Two-Party Contests: Persistent Divergence of Party Positions." *Social Choice and Welfare* 26 (3): 547–69.

Palmer, Maxwell, and Benjamin Schneer. 2016. "Capitol Gains: The Returns to Elected Office from Corporate Board Directorships." *Journal of Politics* 78 (1): 181–96.

———. 2018. "Post-Political Careers: How Politicians Capitalize on Public Office." Working paper, Boston University.

Patty, John W. 2008. "Equilibrium Party Government." *American Journal of Political Science* 52 (3): 636–55.

Pildes, Richard H. 2011. "Why the Center Does Not Hold: The Causes of Hyperpolarized Democracy in America." *California Law Review* 99 (2): 273–333.

Poole, Keith T., and Howard Rosenthal. 1985. "A Spatial Model for Legislative Roll Call Analysis." *American Journal of Political Science* 29 (2): 357–84.

———. 2000. *Congress: A Political-Economic History of Roll Call Voting*. New York: Oxford University Press.

Preece, Jessica, and Olga Stoddard. 2015. "Why Women Don't Run: Experimental Evidence on Gender Differences in Political Competition Aversion." *Journal of Economic Behavior and Organization* 117:296–308.

Prior, Markus. 2003. "Any Good News in Soft News? The Impact of Soft News Preference on Political Knowledge." *Political Communication* 20 (2): 149–71.

Querubín, Pablo, and James M. Snyder Jr. 2013. "The Control of Politicians in Normal Times and Times of Crisis: Wealth Accumulation by U.S. Congressmen, 1850–1880." *Quarterly Journal of Political Science* 8 (4): 409–50.

Rohde, David W. 1991. *Parties and Leaders in the Post-Reform House.* Chicago: University of Chicago Press.

Rosenfeld, Sam. 2017. *The Polarizers: Postwar Architects of Our Partisan Era.* Chicago: University of Chicago Press.

Sabato, Larry J. 1993. *Feeding Frenzy: How Attack Journalism Has Transformed American Politics.* New York: Free Press.

Sanbonmatsu, Kira. 2010. *Where Women Run: Gender and Party in the American States.* Ann Arbor: University of Michigan Press.

Schlesinger, Joseph A. 1966. *Ambition and Politics: Political Careers in the United States.* Chicago: Rand McNally.

Shepsle, Kenneth A. 1978. *The Giant Jigsaw Puzzle: Democratic Committee Assignments in the Modern House.* Chicago: University of Chicago Press.

Shor, Boris, and Nolan McCarty. 2011. "The Ideological Mapping of American Legislatures." *American Political Science Review* 105 (3): 530–51.

Snyder, James M. Jr. 1992. "Long-Term Investing in Politicians; or, Give Early, Give Often." *Journal of Law and Economics* 35 (1): 15–43.

Snyder, Jason. 2005. "Detecting Manipulation in U.S. House Elections." Manuscript, University of California, Los Angeles, last modified January 2005. PDF. http://citeseerx.ist.psu.edu/viewdoc/download?doi=10.1.1.335.6505&rep=rep1 &type=pdf.

Squire, Peverill. 2012. *The Evolution of American Legislatures: Colonies, Territories, and States, 1619–2009.* Ann Arbor: University of Michigan Press.

Stone, Walter J., and Elizabeth N. Simas. 2010. "Candidate Valence and Ideological Positions in U.S. House Elections." *American Journal of Political Science* 54 (2): 371–88.

Sutter, Daniel. 2006. "Media Scrutiny and the Quality of Public Officials." *Public Choice* 129 (1–2): 25–40.

Tausanovitch, Chris, and Christopher Warshaw. 2013. "Measuring Constituent Policy Preferences in Congress, State Legislatures, and Cities." *Journal of Politics* 75 (2): 330–42.

———. 2014. "Representation in Municipal Government." *American Political Science Review* 108 (3): 605–41.

———. 2017. "Estimating Candidates' Political Orientation in a Polarized Congress." *Political Analysis* 25 (2): 167–87.

Theriault, Sean M. 2008. Party Polarization in Congress. New York: Cambridge University Press.

Thomsen, Danielle M. 2014. "Ideological Moderates Won't Run: How Party Fit Matters for Partisan Polarization in Congress." *Journal of Politics* 76 (7): 786–97.

————. 2015. "Why So Few (Republican) Women? Explaining the Partisan Imbalance of Women in the U.S. Congress." *Legislative Studies Quarterly* 40 (2): 295–323.

————. 2017. *Opting Out of Congress: Partisan Polarization and the Decline of Moderate Candidates.* Cambridge: Cambridge University Press.

Tomz, Michael, and Robert P. Van Houweling. 2008. "Candidate Positioning and Voter Choice." *American Political Science Review* 102 (3): 303–18.

Tweedledee5. 2014. "Crush the GOP, Don't Compromise with 'Em—How to Win in 2016 (And What Not to Do). *Daily Kos* (blog), November 5, 2014. http://www .dailykos.com/story/2014/11/5/1342347/-CRUSH-the-GOP-don-t-compromise -with-em-how-to-win-in-2016-and-what-not-to-do.

U.S. Census Bureau. 2017. "Income, Poverty, and Health Insurance Coverage in the United States, 2016." Press release no. CB17-156, September 12, 2017. https:// www.census.gov/newsroom/press-releases/2017/income-povery.html.

Voorheis, John, Nolan McCarty, and Boris Shor. 2015. "Unequal Incomes, Ideology and Gridlock: How Rising Inequality Increases Political Polarization." Working paper.

Warren, Mark. 2014. "Help, We're in a Living Hell and Don't Know How to Get Out." *Esquire*, October 15, 2015. http://www.esquire.com/news-politics/news/a23553 /congress-living-hell-1114/.

Wickline, Michael R. 2010. "Elliott Calls Wills' Mailer a Distraction from Issues." *Arkansas Democrat-Gazette*, June 2.

Williams, Juan. 2010. "Commentary: Tea Party Anger Reflects Mainstream Concerns." *Wall Street Journal*, last updated April 2, 2010. http://www.wsj.com/articles /SB10001424052702304252704575155942054483252.

Index

Chicago Studies in American Politics

A SERIES EDITED BY BENJAMIN I. PAGE, SUSAN HERBST,
LAWRENCE R. JACOBS, AND ADAM J. BERINSKY

IN TIME OF WAR: UNDERSTANDING AMERICAN PUBLIC OPINION FROM WORLD WAR II TO IRAQ *by Adam J. Berinsky*

US AGAINST THEM: ETHNOCENTRIC FOUNDATIONS OF AMERICAN OPINION *by Donald R. Kinder and Cindy D. Kam*

THE PARTISAN SORT: HOW LIBERALS BECAME DEMOCRATS AND CONSERVATIVES BECAME REPUBLICANS *by Matthew Levendusky*

DEMOCRACY AT RISK: HOW TERRORIST THREATS AFFECT THE PUBLIC *by Jennifer L. Merolla and Elizabeth J. Zechmeister*

AGENDAS AND INSTABILITY IN AMERICAN POLITICS, SECOND EDITION *by Frank R. Baumgartner and Bryan D. Jones*

THE PRIVATE ABUSE OF THE PUBLIC INTEREST *by Lawrence D. Brown and Lawrence R. Jacobs*

THE PARTY DECIDES: PRESIDENTIAL NOMINATIONS BEFORE AND AFTER REFORM *by Marty Cohen, David Karol, Hans Noel, and John Zaller*

SAME SEX, DIFFERENT POLITICS: SUCCESS AND FAILURE IN THE STRUGGLES OVER GAY RIGHTS *by Gary Mucciaroni*